5-10-76

REFLECTED GLORY

REFLECTED GLORY

GLORY

THE SPIRIT IN CHRIST AND CHRISTIANS

by
Thomas A. Smail

William B. Eerdmans Publishing Company

Library of Congress Cataloging in Publication Data
Smail, Thomas A   1928-
   Reflected glory.
   Bibliography: p. 157.
   1. Holy Spirit.   I. Title
BT121.2.S56   1975   231'.3   76-968
ISBN 0-8028-3484-1

To Truda

Contents

Preface

WHAT FOLLOWS springs from my own attempt to understand the fresh experience of the Holy Spirit which, almost ten years ago, began to transform my life and ministry, and that continues to be somewhere near the centre for me today. On the one hand I was not content with the theological frameworks that were offered me for its interpretation, and on the other, I was as convinced as ever of the general soundness of the theological approach I had maintained since student days, and this book is the result of an attempt to bring the new experience and the well-tried theology together.

What that theology is will not be hard for the discerning to discover, nor will it be hard to deduce that I have written from the midst of a practical ministry. I hope that the book may be none the worse for that, but it does mean that, while I have tried to keep in touch with what others have written, there are many scholarly questions into which I have been unable to enter, although I am aware that they have been asked and need to be answered. I have come to grips with those opponents who stood in my path, but otherwise have been content to go my way, not looking too far to right or left.

What results is no more than an outline of a theological understanding of the work of the Spirit in Christ and us. Much remains to be filled in and argued through, and perhaps I shall return to the task another day. In the meantime I venture to share what I have seen, in the hope that it may help many throughout the Church who, like me, want to think about what has happened to them in the Spirit.

I myself have been helped not only by the theological authorities whose names appear most frequently in the book, but by the comments and encouragement of my good friend Douglas McBain and my colleague and close companion Michael Harper; by my secretary, Sylvia Lawton and Jean Woolley who typed the manuscript, and most of all by my wife, who, while I have been writing, as always, has held everything together for me.

I pray that the Lord who is the Spirit may have some use for what we have produced to reflect his glory among his people.

London, 1975   THOMAS A. SMAÏL

CHAPTER ONE

Where the Spirit Moves

WHEN THE Holy Spirit moves, the destination is more important than the emotion, what we feel matters less than where we are going. We tend to be more concerned with the Spirit than he is with himself; we can concentrate too much on his activity in us, when he is striving to point us to the origin and the end, in which that activity has its source and significance.

In our day, God is moving with renewing energy in many parts of the Church, and to those who know that renewal from the inside, one of its most fascinating characteristics is that the Spirit brings people into a whole new world of experience of himself, and then completely refuses to let them rest content either with the experience itself, or with himself as the immediate author of it. The personal and corporate new births he generates, the resurrections he arranges, the moral fruits he matures, the charismatic gifts he imparts—are in themselves fascinating phenomena, which those who experience them rightly find exciting, engrossing, fulfilling and refreshing. When that kind of thing happens to you, your impulse is to go out and testify about it, and your temptation in that testimony is to concentrate on what has happened to you in and for itself, and to be not too interested in its wider implications, still less in its theological significance. To combine a concentration on the outpourings of immediate enthusiasm with a disdain of doctrinal reflection has been a pressing temptation of Christian renewal movements down the centuries.

But where the Spirit has been in control that temptation has not had its way. Because of his own nature, the Holy Spirit will soon exert pressure upon us to seek the source from which our experiences and gifts have come, the norm by which they are to be judged, and the end which they are meant to serve. And he will exert this pressure, not because he wants to make us all theologians —which, thank God, he does not—but because he wants to make and keep us all Christians, that is, people who know that everything about them, and their spiritual experiences most of all, have their source and standard and significance in the person and work of Christ.

The Spirit moves us towards Christ. He does this because, according to the New Testament, his nature is such that he cannot be spoken of by himself or sought for himself. He has his own distinct and indispensable life, not in any independence of his own, but within the mysterious community of the Godhead. He lives and acts totally and entirely as the one who, as the Nicene Creed puts it, proceeds from the Father and the Son and whose entire ministry and service is to glorify the Father and the Son.

His work among God's people is in conformity with his position in God's being. The Holy Spirit does not do his own thing, which is somehow in a realm by itself apart from the work of Christ, or which is somehow an improvement or advance upon the work of Christ. The one who in his being proceeds from Father and Son, can only do a work which glorifies Father and Son. This is the clear teaching of Jesus in the crucial verses John 16: 12–15, which are quite normative for any Christian understanding of the Spirit, and to which we shall have to return again and again. "He will not speak on his own authority but whatever he hears, he will speak . . . He will glorify me, for he will take what is mine, and declare it to you." The Holy Spirit has nothing of his own to declare or bring us. Jesus says: "All that the Father has is mine"—so that there is no autonomous glory of the Spirit apart from the one glory of the

Lord, and the work of the Spirit is simply to take what is given in Christ and to make it event and experience for his people. "Therefore I said that he will take what is mine and declare it to you."

The Church of Scotland Panel on Doctrine Report is therefore on good New Testament ground when it questions the trinitarian orthodoxy of any Pentecostalism in which "The Holy Spirit, while not exactly replacing Christ is acting independently of and in addition to what Christ has done and is doing," (1) and when it insists positively that "Reformed theology has always affirmed that the primary work of the Holy Spirit is to reveal the risen and living Christ, the only Lord and Saviour, to his Church and people." (2)

To follow out some of the implications of that Christ-wards bent of the Spirit is the main purpose of this book. But for the moment it is important to dwell a little on the preliminary point, that what we have outlined so far is not simply an orthodox trinitarian understanding of the Spirit, or a statement of the central New Testament doctrine about his place in the gospel, it is a description of the way that he actually works again and again in the experience of people who are open to him. When he is set free in the Church, he will first of all generate fresh experiences of every New Testament kind and variety. There will be personal conversions and corporate resurrections and illuminatings and empowerings and sanctifyings, and things will happen among God's people that will make them exclaim with wonder that "the Lord has done great things for us; we are glad" (Ps. 126:3). Where that wonder and gladness are absent it is doubtful if the Spirit is freely at work. But the wonder and the gladness will, again if the Spirit is working freely, not be allowed to distract us from the main emphasis, that it is the Lord who has done these great things. The two great aspects of his work are to make great things happen, and then to show them to be Christ's things, coming from the Lord.

The way that the Spirit first generates experience, and then in that experience moves us towards Christ, can be illustrated from within the New Testament itself by outlining the development of its teaching on the Spirit as presented first in Acts and then in Paul. In Acts, while the sending of the Spirit is seen right from the start as the work of Christ, the Spirit is most closely connected with the remarkable experiences and events which he brings about. In the wind and fire of Pentecost, in the tongues that gathered the crowds, in the shaking of the house where the apostles sat, in the strange events that led Peter to the house of Cornelius and Philip to the eunuch's chariot—the Spirit is most evidently present, and these things are the signs and evidences of his presence. The strange story of the Samaritans seems nearly to be saying that an absence of such *charismata* is an absence of the Spirit. Eduard Schweizer sums up Luke's contribution thus: "The peculiarity of Luke's testimony lies in its demonstration that a Church which has no special power to fulfil its concrete missionary task is a Church without the Spirit". (3)

This is one of the things which the contemporary charismatic movement is saying to the Church, because it has found that the Spirit who brought about the events and experiences which Luke relates is ready to be active in similar ways in the Church today. It is in fact this kind of event which alerts the Church again and again to the fact that there is working within it a power that is not its own power, doing to it and through it what it could not do for itself.

But for the final New Testament word about the Spirit, we have to go beyond Luke to Paul. Paul goes back on nothing that Luke has said. The gifts and activities of the Spirit are all still recognised, "The Spirit is still the miraculous power which proceeds entirely from God, and breaks in upon man's affairs in a way quite out of his control." (4) But for Paul the Spirit does not merely have his source in Christ and come forth from him to do dramatic deeds. For Paul "the Lord is the Spirit" (2 Cor. 3:17), the entire content of the work of the Spirit is to minister Christ, his basic work to bring men to the confession "Jesus is Lord" (1 Cor. 12:3). "The Spirit is the power of God which enables a man to believe in the cross and resurrection of Jesus." (5) The gifts of the Spirit are those which build up the Church to operate as Christ's Body, the Spirit's fruit is that which realises Christ's likeness in Christ's people, his work is so dependent upon and identified with the work of Christ that he can be regularly referred to as the Spirit of Christ (Rom. 8:9).

This insight into the close connection between Christ and Spirit means that the extent of the Spirit's work can be more clearly recognised. If, with Luke, we tend to identify the activity of the Spirit somewhat exclusively with obviously miraculous experiences and gifts, we shall regard the Spirit's work in too restricted a way. But for Paul and developed New Testament teaching, the identification of Christ and Spirit is seen in a much wider context. Christ does indeed operate by his Spirit where there are tongues and healings and prophecies, but his power which manifestly operates in these outstanding gifts, is in fact the source of the whole Christian experience in all its aspects, however undramatic some of them may seem. The signs and wonders simply jolt us awake afresh to the constant activity of the risen Christ among his people, so that we come to see the creativity and transforming power of his Spirit not just where the signs are given, but in the total range of Christian living. The same power that wonderfully raises the lame man at the temple gate, equally wonderfully goes on realising the new creation in the Church, whereby men in the miracle of faith can receive and confess Christ, and in the miracle of love can enter into new attitudes and relationships to one another and the world.

In other words, the significant thing about the dramatic signs is not their miraculous quality as such, but that they are signs of the activity of the risen Jesus, and they open our eyes to see with fresh clarity that the basis of the whole Christian life in all its personal and corporate dimensions is his renewing work, which is as completely outside our own competence as any of the miracles, and therefore as completely his gift to us.

It is consistent with this that in dealing with the *charismata* Paul makes no distinction between ordinary and extraordinary gifts. He has no miracle-mongering preference for the dramatic gifts of 1 Corinthians 12 and equally no 'anti-supernaturalist' prejudice in favour of the more 'ordinary' gifts of Romans 12, and in fact makes no distinction between the two. Prophecy, healing, and the working of miracles have no less permanent a place in the life of Christ's Body than service, liberality, teaching and exhortation. On the other hand the latter as much as the former are charismatic, they are not just natural human talents dedicated to Christ, they are the gracious giving of new possibilities to our renewed humanity, and they are gifts of the Spirit because they do what dedicated human talents by themselves never could do; they have transcendent reference, and they reveal and convey the power and presence of the ascended Lord. One set of gifts is never played off against the other. The presence of prophecy in both lists shows that for Paul they are on the same footing, because the criterion by which they are accepted as gifts of the Spirit is that Christ is manifested by the Spirit in all of them.

Even such a general outline of how New Testament understanding of the Spirit develops from Acts to Paul shows how attention is turned from the Spirit as the generator of mighty works, to the Spirit, as the agent of Christ, making real in the disciples all that was real in the Master. The particular manifestations of the Spirit that mark his Pentecostal breakthrough, while themselves seen as continuing and permanent aspects of Christian experience, help to open the way for the understanding of the whole of the Christian life as the scene of charismatic activity, in all its parts the result of the gracious renewing work of Christ's grace.

This movement from experience to its source and norm in Christ takes place within the New Testament, not as a process of religious sophistication, a taming of the primitive into the balanced, nor as a process of doctrinal evolution, but as a result of the Spirit's active working in those who have received him, so that he reveals himself as the one who takes what was objectively done for us by Christ and brings it to experienced event within us, and does this in order that in the Church's experience of its new life, Christ who is the source of that life may be glorified.

All this is of very much more than biblical or historical interest. As the Spirit moved the first Christians from the experiences they had received to the Christ who had sent them, so whenever he moves renewingly in the Church, we should expect the same process to be repeated. My own concern is to assert that this process can be seen as being repeated within that contemporary movement of the Holy Spirit variously known as neo-Pentecostalism and the charismatic renewal. Among those who have been radically affected by this movement—and here I have to speak as a participator rather than an observer—there can be traced a similar development, so that some of us have started with experiences like those recorded in Acts and have been moved on to an understanding of them very like Paul's.

For such, charismatic renewal characteristically begins, as it began in Acts, with a transforming encounter with the Holy Spirit as the generator and immediate source of new religious experiences and events, as the one whose new outpouring is associated with a very vivid personal or corporate renewal in the life of an individual or church, and often with the operation of those spiritual gifts which most clearly and evidently proclaim themselves to be not natural human capabilities, but signs of the direct activity of God. This vivid experience accompanied by the exercise of a charismatic gift, typically but not necessarily the gift of tongues, is the typical shape of what has, under Pentecostal influence, come to be called 'baptism in the Holy Spirit'. We shall have a good deal more to say about this emotive and controversial phrase before we are finished, but at the moment it is enough to note initially, that it is a conscious and often intense spiritual experience that it describes.

I write as one for whom just such an experience can be seen, in the perspective of almost ten years, to have been a quite critical turning point. It was a dateable event which moved a man and a ministry from a position of relatively fruitless effortfulness and existential distance from God, into releasing discovery of the limitless life and power that God sought to make available to me, of the largely unappropriated reality of praise and prayer, of a new sense of being personally addressed by the word of God in scripture, a new pastoral empathy with people and a new ability to diagnose and deal with their needs, a new confidence and reality in preaching and worship, and a new sense of victory at some outstanding points of defeat in the moral struggle—all leading to a new confidence of hope in what God was going to do in my own life and in the life of his Church.

All these things I had long known as the content of New Testament faith and promise; my attitude to them was one of openness precisely because I knew that they were taught and promised in the gospel and so were integrally related to Christ. If I had not been convinced that Christ was its source, I would certainly not have opened myself to the experience that came to me, so that the Christocentricity of the whole matter was implicit in it from the start, just as in Acts.

But the distinctive and new factor that being 'baptised in the Spirit' brings is not apprehension or understanding of the truth, but rather the generation of experience so that a man who has entered into it does not want to say primarily "This is the truth" but rather first and foremost "This has happened to me."

Charismatics in the first fine careless rapture of their newfound renewal are a little like the healed blind man in John 9. They are as aware as he was that the great change that has come about in them has its source in Jesus, and that it has its greatest significance in the new depth of relationship with Jesus that it inaugurates, but first of all it is the new experience of sight itself that excites and engrosses him, so that he keeps trying to escape from all the puzzling questions about how all this relates to Jesus, that others seek to thrust upon him, back to the one thing he is sure of, and that will ultimately lead him to the answers about Jesus as well.

"The answers to all your questions about the one that healed me I do not know: one thing I know that, though I was blind, now I see" (John 9:25). That is why the first literature of revivalist movements, and so of the charismatic renewal is testimony literature, which does indeed seek to authenticate itself in New Testament terms, but whose chief burden is to say: "This is what the Holy Spirit has done in me."

The potential perils of such a condition are many. Chief among them is that a man, who is excited by his vivid experience of the Spirit and his gifts, is in danger of suggesting that the activity of the Holy Spirit is confined to this kind of experience and these kinds of gifts, that in being baptised in the Spirit and speaking in tongues he has 'received' the Spirit and those who 'only' believe in Christ, and have not had all this happen to them, are in a lesser and perhaps even dubious relationship to the Holy Spirit. So are generated all the divisions between the 'haves' and 'have-nots', those 'first-class' Christians who feel that now they have the Holy Spirit and those 'second-class' Christians who are made to feel that they have not.

People who have recently entered into a revitalising experience of the Holy Spirit are like a newly married couple on their honeymoon. They are not always the best company, because they have no eyes for anything or anybody, their one engrossing concern to explore and enjoy the new thing that has happened to them. The last thing that you could expect, or with reason require of them, is balance and a sense of proportion.

So charismatics in the first flush of their new thing can be a great trial to the more sober Christians around them. They tend to go on and on about the Holy Spirit, what he has done in them and the gifts he has opened to them, till people feel that one aspect of the faith has taken over from all the others, and that the Christian centralities have been ousted by a peripheral concern with experiences and gifts that are not all that clearly related to Jesus Christ, incarnate and crucified, and to the tasks and concerns of his gospel and kingdom.

If things were to stay like that, then such Christians might remain literally eccentric—people off-centre in their faith. Sometimes they do stay like that; just as there are married people who try to pretend the honeymoon is still on when it is long over, so there are Christians who are afraid to go on to maturity, and try to prolong the thrill of their first days in the Spirit when that thrill has inevitably and rightly faded. For honeymooners have to come home, they are not allowed to keep the new thing in isolation but have to begin to relate it to the abiding centralities of life, family and work and community and have—perhaps painfully—to adjust afresh to them. So, if they will follow the further leading of the Spirit who has blessed them, provision is made for the home-coming of eccentric charismatics—bringing their new blessings with them. They have to begin to relate what has happened to them in the Spirit to the wholeness of the faith and the life of the Church to which it belongs. The Holy Spirit, operating within the Body of Christ, sees to it that his own Christ-centred bias appears in those whom he is filling, and that the experience that had its source in Christ will have the effect of leading the man to whom it has happened back to Christ.

The sphere in which this sometimes becomes first apparent is that of worship. Many Christians have come to charismatic gatherings and heard testimonies and witnessed the exercise of spiritual gifts that in themselves would have bewildered and perhaps even dismayed them, and yet the whole thing has in fact commended itself to them and impressed them, because the dominant effect of what has happened to the people involved in it is to release them into a new warmth of praise in which the glory of the Father and of his Son, Jesus Christ, is most rejoicingly celebrated. The typical charismatic song is the objective proclamation of the central New Testament fact, with all the subjective warmth of those who have made personal discovery of it, and so sing "Jesus is Lord."

In the same way the Spirit leads people out of their subjectivity into a new understanding of how the gifts of the Spirit have their significance only in terms of the upbuilding of Christ's Body for doing Christ's corporate work; out of their individualism to an exploration of Christian community, of how in very practical costly and down-to-earth ways Christians may share together the life that Christ puts in them by his Spirit, and to see that the only context in which the Spirit and his power have any meaning is in relation to our witness and evangelism.

Concentration on personal religious experiences as such could shut us up in holy huddles where we edify ourselves and seek new sensations, but it is surely significant that today in the second decade of charismatic renewal the key concerns are not with tongues and individual blessing, but with the practical rediscovery of Christian community and what it means to be the Body of Christ. It is these factors that give renewal its present shape and purpose. More and more it becomes clear, wherever the Spirit is working freely, that his work has its source in Christ, finds its nature in our relationship to Christ, and has its end and purpose in the glory of Christ. The charismatic renewal can come to maturity only as it begins to show to the Church that it can "grow up in every way into him who is the head, into Christ" (Eph. 4:15).

To concentrate on speaking with tongues can be divisive and seemingly eccentric, but to say 'Jesus is Lord' is to emphasise that which is universally Christian and therefore tends to unite all believers. In the New Testament, as we have seen, Christians began with outstanding experiences and gifts of the Spirit, which plainly proclaimed themselves as the signs of the living Christ in the midst of his people, and, in the light of that, they went on to see the whole basis and outworking of Christian discipleship as that which the Holy Spirit alone could render possible and actual, so that the whole individual and corporate life of Christians had a charismatic quality about it, and could never come into being as a natural human possibility but only as a new creation by Christ in the power of the Spirit.

So today the contribution of the charismatic renewal to the Church is not to separate off some people as charismatics in relation to others who are not. Just as the only justification for evangelical or catholic movements is to remind the whole Church that it is at its very basis evangelical or catholic, and they become divisive when they arrogate the adjective exclusively to themselves and deny it to others; so the contribution of the charismatics is to remind the whole Church that it is basically charismatic, that its whole life is to be concrete and miraculous manifestation of the renewing grace of Christ.

It is good that the Church should be awakened to fresh dimensions of the Spirit's operation and to long neglected gifts like prophecy and healing and tongues and the rest, but it is better still that those who have experienced these things should, out of that experience, be available to make the whole Church aware that everything about the Church, Christian existence, Christian knowledge, Christian confession, Christian character, Christian community, Christian worship—all these have their basis in the operation of the Holy Spirit expressing Christ's life in free creativity among his people.

But if charismatic renewal is to be unitive and upbuilding and renewing within the Church, it must itself be moved by the Spirit from everything sectarian and fanatical and eccentric within it, and this involves a ceaseless discipline of thinking about the work of the Spirit in its relation to the person and work of Christ. Thus the charismatic renewal has to supplement testimony with theology —not to prove its intellectual competence—but to understand itself, and to let others understand it, as proceeding from and tending towards the one who alone can authenticate anything as Christian —the Lord Jesus Christ himself. Only in Christ can this work of the Spirit achieve solidity, gain acceptance, promote unity and advance renewal.

Thus in answer to our question "Where does the Spirit move us?" our answer must be "Through the experiences that he gives us back to the Christ whose glory he seeks to manifest in his Body." This book seeks, from the point of view of one immersed in the current charismatic renewal, and as such concerned more than ever for the centrality of Christ, to explore the work of the Holy Spirit, in order to show in detail the vital connection between spiritual experience and the person and work of Christ; in so doing to establish charismatic experience on the one foundation that can uphold it, to commend it to the Church as an integral and authentic articulation of the gospel, by showing that the charismatic renewal has to be as centred on Christ in its thinking and witnessing as it is already in its praise.

Notes to Chapter One

NOTES

1 Report of the Panel on Doctrine, *The Charismatic Movement within the Church of Scotland* (1974) p. 4

2 Ibid. p. 4

3 Eduard Schweizer, *Spirit of God* (translated from Kittel's *Theologisches Wörterbuch zum Neuen Testament*), (Adam and Charles Black, 1960), p. 50

4 Ibid. p. 80

5 Ibid. p. 81

CHAPTER TWO

Into His Likeness

WE HAVE defined the role of the Holy Spirit in a twofold way, as
both generating the experience of Christians and promoting the
glory of Christ. We shall clarify what is involved in both these
aspects of his work, and also the relationship between them, if we
try to think them through in greater detail with the help of one of
Paul's central statements about the person and place of the Spirit
in 2 Corinthians 3:18, where he says "And we all with unveiled
face, beholding (R.S.V. margin, reflecting) the glory of the Lord,
are being changed into his likeness from one degree of glory to
another; for this comes from the Lord, who is the Spirit."

From the wealth of richness in this single verse, we should note
the following central points:

1 There is here the closest identification of the Lord (*Kurios*) and
the Spirit (*Pneuma*). This is clear from the last phrase, and is even
more explicit in verse 17, "Now the Lord is the Spirit and where
the Spirit of the Lord is, there is liberty." Most commentators
agree that Paul is not here asserting a metaphysical identity of
being between two divine persons, which would oblige us to
abbreviate our trinitarianism into a binitarianism. Schweizer
rightly remarks that in the New Testament the ontological question
"how God, Lord and Spirit are related to each other is not yet felt

to be a question at all." (1) In any case *Kurios*, Lord, is the characteristic title, not of the Holy Spirit, but of Jesus Christ. But when, as here, Paul is thinking of the experience of the Church in the Spirit, then he recognises that that experience has its distinctive quality and significance from the fact that in it we again encounter the Lord, not now as the one who is incarnate *among* us, or who has died and risen *for* us, but as the one who comes as Spirit to live and act *within* us, to take what has been shown to us and done for us and make it happen *in* us. There is here a dynamic identification and a practical coincidence of the work of the *Lord* and the work of the *Spirit*—the *Lord* is the *Spirit*. There could be no clearer indication of how basic and central a Christological understanding of the Spirit's work is in the New Testament, and this must be equally central and basic in all we say. We shall know that we are talking rightly of the Spirit, when we discover that we are still talking about the Lord.

2   In this verse we can identify an original prototype from which a reflected image is in process of being made. The prototype is "the glory of the Lord" (*doxa Kuriou*), and the copy is the "likeness" (*eikon*) into which "we are being changed", so that the glory which is original to him, is refracted and reflected in us. The copy is made by exposure to the original. It is by beholding his glory that we begin to be changed into his likeness.

The Greek participle, *katoptrizomenoi*, can be variously translated "contemplating" or "reflecting". R.S.V. opts for the first rendering and notes the second in the margin. N.E.B. chooses the second, with some justification, since the meaning "to reflect in a mirror" fits in well with the word *eikon*, likeness, which follows. In fact both meanings mark out distinctive aspects of the Christian's relationship to Christ. First of all he looks away from himself, turns towards (v. 16), and with unveiled face beholds (v. 18) the Lord, sees that in him which is original to him. But as he thus looks to Christ and opens himself to him, the knowledge of Christ that he gains is never simply objective and intellectual knowledge, it is knowledge that begins to change him, so that he begins to reflect that to which he has been exposed, and its likeness begins to be formed in him.

In other words, concentration on Christ, unveiled openness to Christ, faith in Christ is the presupposition of everything that follows from it; but what does follow from it is real Christian experience. Faith in Christ puts us in the place where experience of Christ may start.

This experience is actualised by the Spirit. It happens "as by the Lord who is the Spirit". He is the active medium, the light in between the two, which carries what is in the original and makes it appear again in reflection in the likeness.

3   The original is described as "the glory of the Lord" (*doxa Kuriou*). Glory means here the revealed person, character, work and power of the Lord Jesus Christ. It is the revelation of the sum of the love, truth, saving grace and power, which are hidden from the world and from the veiled face of unbelieving Israel (v. 14), but are revealed to all who turn and believe in him (v. 16). The element of *revealed* brightness, of *manifested* majesty is quite essential to the word glory. In the light of the resurrection, we have seen the secret hidden in all his works and ways from Jordan to Calvary—"we have beheld his glory, full of grace and truth" (John 1:14).

But that glory, although from the point of view of our Christian experience it is original to him, is also "glory as of the only Son from the Father" (John 1:14). It is "the glory of the Lord" and as he derives the title, Lord, from his Father and shares it with him, so he is the Mediator of the glory of God—of the grace, love, truth and power which have their ultimate origin not in himself but in his Father. In him the glory of God becomes accessible and available to us, "No one has ever seen God; the only Son, who is in the bosom of the Father, he has made him known" (John 1:18).

Thus the work of the Holy Spirit is, as it were, only the last stage in a great divine descent, involving at each stage a munificent mediation. The power and glory belong to the Father, but are mediated to mankind in the Son—and are then transferred to us and reflected in us by the Spirit. The glory is from the Father, through the Son and in the Spirit. In the Son the glory becomes humanly perceptible and available—he is himself the "image (*eikon* = likeness) of the invisible God" (Col. 1:15) and "he reflects the glory of God" (Heb. 1:3), so that the New Testament uses the very same words to describe Christ's reflected likeness of the Father, as Paul uses here to describe our reflected likeness of Christ. In the Spirit "our fellowship (*koinonia* = shared life) is with the Father and with his Son, Jesus Christ" (1 John 1:3).

4   The making of the copy is thus described, "We are being changed into his likeness from one degree of glory to another" (*apo doxes eis doxan*). This is the nature of the experience that the Spirit generates in us as we look to Christ. In some ways the word 'event' would be better than the word 'experience', with all its subjective connotations. What the Holy Spirit does in us is in its degree as real and factual, as what Jesus has done for us. It has only peripherally to do with the generation of feeling, the stirring of subjectivity, the moving of emotion; it has centrally to do with a change in the whole shape and form (*morphe*) of our living and personality. When we look to Christ, whatever we feel with our emotions, something begins to happen to us, we are being changed, literally "meta-morphosed", we used to be in one *morphe*, but now we are coming into another.

A good deal can be learnt about the nature of this change, and of our Christian experience simply by parsing the verb—*metamorphoumetha* (we are being changed) which Paul uses,

(a) It is present continuous in tense. There is no question here of one great change being once and for all completed—it is not an aorist. There is a decisive turning to Christ involving a critical change at the beginning of the Christian life, but that is not what Paul is talking about here. There is a being glorified at the end of the Christian life which is entirely future—but that is not in question here. This is a present and progressive being conformed to Christ in which here and now many degrees of his glory—

many manifestations of his grace and truth and love and power —begin to appear in us, so that already, far short of heaven, we can be said to move from glory to glory. There is no suggestion here of any static 'arrived' Christianity, but rather a dynamic, ceaseless and progressive reflection of the Lord.

(b) The verb is passive in mood. This change is not something which we do, but always something that is done to us, as we open ourselves in faith to the Lord. Even the faith, in which we do that, is not a work or attainment that has its source in ourselves, but is itself the work of the Holy Spirit in us through the gospel. Many of us who have known well that the forgiveness of sins and the opening of the kingdom of heaven were the gifts of Christ's grace to which we contributed nothing, have nevertheless striven by human effort to change our lives, the life of the Church and even the life of the world, so that they would become places where the glory of the Lord was reflected. It has taken us a long time to discover that it could not happen that way, for it is grace that transforms and not human effort, and that applies to every aspect of the Christian life from the very beginning to the very end. In one aspect of its witness, the charismatic renewal is simply calling us to consistency, and reminding us that, unless God does his changing work in us, we shall be unable to change anything for him.

(c) The verb is plural in number. It is *we* who are being changed. The work of the Holy Spirit is by no means confined to what is inward and individual; his typical place of operation is the corporate fellowship of the Church. It is not given to any one person to reflect more than a little of the Lord's glory. Each individual Christian can be nothing more than one in a circle of many mirrors set round a great central light. Each has its own glint of brightness, the reflection that is appropriate from that angle and in that situation, but it takes all the mirrors in right relationship to one another to reflect the brightness of the light from every angle. So the complete glory of Christ can be exhibited only in the complete Body of his people, as the Spirit reflects him, personally but not individualistically, deeply but not privately in the life that they share. The adequate mirror of Christ's glory can only be the whole Church of God.

5   But the sum of all we have said is to insist that this glory appears not only in Christ but in us. However pale and insignificant in comparison with the prototype, the likeness is still real and authentic, and has its own share of glory. The change in us is "from glory to glory". Just as Christ's glory could be beheld by all who had eyes to see, and, if they could not see, it was because of their inherent blindness rather than his inherent hiddenness, so the reflected glory of Christ in the Church will have outer visible form. Its content is the "manifestation (*phanerosis*) of the Spirit" which is given to each (1 Cor. 12:7), the things that Christ has poured out which can be seen and heard (Acts 2:33) and the concretely and outwardly expressed life of the Christian community, the Body of Christ (1 Cor. 12). The Spirit must not be 'spiritualised'. He operates in the Body and his business there is to produce visible glory, which all who have eyes for reality can see.

This one verse—2 Corinthians 3:18, has provided us with a setting within which we may profitably try to comprehend the work of the Spirit in all its New Testament dimensions. The Holy Spirit is engaged in a dynamic mediation that has its starting place in the glory of Christ and its destination in the experience of the community of believers. This is in the end the most profound thing that can be said of him—he changes us into the likeness of the Lord.

The next thing that we need to notice is that the human means by which the Spirit accomplishes our transformation into Christ is our faith. This is implicit in the passage we have been studying. It is not all and sundry who are being changed into Christ's likeness, but a group ('we'), who can, in principle, be defined as those who have, in the language of the passage, "turned to the Lord with unveiled face"—that is, a group of believers. The whole transformation that we have been describing takes place within the realm of faith, it is through faith that it is both realised and recognised. What we do not believe of Christ, we cannot go on to experience of Christ. Faith is the human means, the Jacob's ladder, that the Spirit constructs in order to do his work in us; it is the door that the Spirit opens so that we may have access to Christ and he to us; as Calvin once put it, faith is the empty hand that we hold out to Christ and that he fills with himself, and the impulse and strength to stretch out the hand come from the Spirit, and it is the Spirit who through our faith fills us with Christ.

Thus, just as the two poles of the Spirit's activity are the Christ he glorifies and the experience of the believer in which he works to create Christ's likeness, so faith, as the means by which the Spirit opens us to himself, has as its sole concern and content God's gift of himself to us in Christ, and as its intended consequence the implanting of Christ's likeness in us. In faith there is involved both a believing and a receiving. This is implied in Paul's question to the twelve disciples at Ephesus, "Did you receive ... when you believed?" (Acts 19:2). Faith has in it both an openness to Christ —a believing—and a taking to ourselves of Christ and all his benefits, a receiving. It is never merely a matter of trusting to Christ who is apart from us, although it must start with that, but through that trust, he comes among us and his likeness is formed manifestly in us. It was because Paul could not see in the twelve at Ephesus any experiential manifestation of Christ, that he argued back to a defect in their faith in Christ.

The question of the relationship between the object in which faith rests and the experience which faith facilitates will occupy us for the next two chapters. As we discuss it we shall also be elucidating the manner in which the Holy Spirit, the inspirer of faith, conforms our experience to Christ. As the matter is complicated and elusive, let us in the first place study it in terms of a concrete New Testament incident where the main features of the relationship are made especially clear.

In John 4:46–54 it is very clear from the whole thrust of the dialogue between Jesus and the official from Capernaum that the means of his son's healing is going to be the father's faith. The course of the healing, and the will and power to perform it are in Jesus, not the father, but the father's faith is the necessary connecting link between his son's need and Jesus's help. The turning point of the passage is obviously verse 50 "Jesus said to him, 'Go; your son will live'. The man believed the word that Jesus spoke to him and went his way." His faith is created by the word that Jesus speaks and the promise that he makes. Implicit in the father's believing obedience is his verdict about Jesus, not theologically formulated, but clearly expressed in what he does. His faith does not rest in any experiential fulfilment of the promise but in what he knows of Christ who has promised. The content of his faith is the Lord alone. Before he sees, he believes.

But having believed, he sees. That which Jesus promises him, "Your son will live" is of such a nature that it can only be fulfilled by a particular happening. And that happening takes place. In response to the believing of the father, there is a receiving of that which Jesus promises by the son. At the hour when Christ's promise created the father's faith, the boy began to mend. The promises of the gospel are such that, when they find faith, they press through to particular fulfilment in experience, in event. The gospel is not in word only but in manifestation of the Spirit and in power. If the father had gone home and found his boy's situation unchanged, he would soon have concluded that there was something mistaken about his believing, because what he had believed had not happened. One of the characteristics of God's word is that what it promises happens when it is believed, and if it does not, it leaves behind a situation of contradiction and unreality. Thus the *object* of faith is Christ, but, because Christ is who he is and promises what he promises, the *end* of faith is experience.

Thus we have to consider what happens when faith is not rightly related either to its Christological object or to its experiential result. Leaving the first concern until the next chapter, we shall pursue the second now. Faith leads to event. Writing of God's vocation of a man to faith and service Karl Barth says,

The vocation of man should not be divested of its concrete historicity nor transcendentalised. We do not speak of it correctly, nor of God as its acting subject, if we speak of it docetically ... We must not present the being and work and Word and Spirit of God as an hypothesis, which, even with great majesty glory, simply hovers over the mind and heart and life of man like a radiant ball of glass or soap-bubbles, but never leads to the result that something happens. (2)

Or, as Elizabeth put it more simply to Mary, "Blessed is she who believed, for there will be a fulfilment of what was spoken to her from the Lord." (Luke 1:45).

The need for the Holy Spirit to bring promise through faith into reality needs to be remembered by those who wish to describe the status and condition of Christians and churches in an objective way based solely upon scriptural statements quite apart from contemporary reality.

For example, F. D. Bruner, in dealing with Acts 2:38 can write "Our text teaches us that since the occurrence of Pentecost, Christian baptism becomes the locus of the Spirit's reception in response to the Spirit's pressure in preaching. Henceforth baptism is Pentecost." (3)

Now this may well be a true interpretation of the purpose of God in baptism and may be a description of standard Christian experience in the New Testament Church—that all those who were baptised entered into a reception and experience of the Spirit parallel to that of the apostles on the day of Pentecost. But to claim that it is a universal theological description of what baptism has been, and must automatically be in the Church is to run into complete unreality. Countless have been baptised both as babies and as believers who have known little of the experience of the outpoured Spirit recorded in the New Testament. No doubt they have in their baptism stood under the same promise, but the question is whether it has been fulfilled, and that can only be answered by considering the experience of the baptised and seeing whether it passes the New Testament tests for what it means to receive the gift of the Holy Spirit. The whole question of the actual level of the Church's spiritual experience and why it has fallen so woefully short of the experience of the first Church, cannot be swept under the carpet by claiming that in the theology of the New Testament there is an essential connection between baptism and Pentecost.

To address the contemporary Church as if every statement made about the Church in scripture were automatically true of it, quite apart from its present state and condition, to tell believers who know themselves to be spiritually inadequate that rivers of living water are pouring from them, to tell those who feel futile and fruitless in their Christian service that the outpoured energy of the Holy Spirit is freely at work in them, to tell Christians who are hardly aware of the Holy Spirit that they are already baptised in the Spirit, solely because the New Testament is interpreted as saying that all Christians are baptised in the Spirit—all this is to run into complete unreality. The New Testament speaks of people being full of the Spirit, or of the Church being baptised in the Spirit, in the light of the actual experience of the churches and people to whom these words were addressed, and they can be applied with reality only to people who have had the same thing happen to them.

Many of the baptised know well that so far their baptism has *not* been Pentecost and, to such people, what Bruner says becomes abstract theologising quite out of touch with things as they are. As John Taylor puts it, to engage in glowing descriptions of the New Testament Church, without showing how the modern Church can become like it, again "is to be thrown into the most painful depression and despair ... We can search in vain among all the churches and sects for anything resembling what is described in the New Testament, let alone what is promised there." (4) The promises of the New Testament cannot just be pinned on to the lapels of believers; they have to become event in their experience, and if they do not, they become remote and theoretical, mere 'theology' that has little practical substantiation, as Barth put it, soap bubbles above our heads that may charm us but never touch us.

Paul's gospel is far from being such a theology. The preaching of the cross at Corinth is no theoretical declaration of a completed justification; being believed, it has results, so that idolaters, adulterers, drunkards and robbers (I Cor. 6:9-10) "were washed, sanctified, justified in the name of the Lord Jesus Christ and in the Spirit of our God" (v. 11). The receiving of the Spirit at Galatia was no automatic doctrinal implication of conversion. Paul can appeal (3:4) to a manifested experience that has included constant supply of the Spirit and the working of miracles among them. At Ephesus the hearing of the word of truth, and their believing of it resulted in their being sealed "with the promised Holy Spirit, which is the guarantee of our inheritance until we acquire possession of it to the praise of his glory" (Eph. 1:13-14). Here is a hearing, that leads to a believing, that in turn is authenticated, sealed and guaranteed by eventful experience.

The experience we have received is not yet the complete replica of Christ the prototype in whom we have believed. This is only the first instalment, but as such it is the guarantee of all the rest to come; our present tasting of Christ enables us to hope expectantly for the still not-yet of our Christian experience. The experienced victory enables us to continue the fight into new territory, the answered prayer helps us to pray on in the still unanswered situation, the down payment guarantees the inheritance.

But it is still true that faith has the authentication of the Spirit's making real in experience what is promised in Christ, if only in a preliminary way. Paul writes not mainly as a theologian spelling out the theoretical consequences of belief in Christ, but as one who described what his first readers were experiencing, whose faith had been vindicated because already they, with him, knew something of the likeness of the Lord and of "the immeasurable greatness of his power in us who believe" (Eph. 1:19).

In our time the Pentecostals have drawn attention again to this scriptural emphasis on Christian experience and the Holy Spirit

as the one who generates that experience. Their theological understanding of the work of the Spirit may need correction, but the
insight that every promise of Christ has at least the beginnings of
its fulfilment here and now in the action of the Holy Spirit through
faith among his people, is utterly biblical and of the very essence of
Christian renewal. John Taylor, commenting upon the Pentecostal
emphasis, says,

1905757

We may be in great need of a rediscovery. For every Christian
is meant to possess his possessions and many never do. The
freedom of a son of God should be not merely a legal title but a
fact of experience, and essentially a shared experience. It is
better to call it incorrectly a second blessing and lay hold of the
reality of new life in Christ, than to let the soundness of our
doctrine rob us of its substance. (5)

So experience is the consequence of faith. To end with a personal
postscript, I was well through my divinity course before the Lord's
Supper meant anything to me. I knew the theology of it in some
of its daunting complication, I knew, as word and promise, all that
it was supposed to mean to me personally. I would sit through the
service and tell myself that all these things were true, and yet
without any consciousness of anything happening. Then one day
at a student retreat, when the sacrament was celebrated in a
billiard room, with the cup came an intense consciousness of being
accepted by Christ, almost as if a voice had spoken the words as I
drank "you are accepted". And by that every subsequent communion has been affected and informed. The sacrament had passed
from being believed to being received. It is when our faith can
break through into real happening, and instead of just affirming a
relationship, can actually start to enjoy it, that the Spirit does his
work and reflects in us the likeness of the Lord.

NOTES
1   Eduard Schweizer, *Spirit of God* p. 84
2   Karl Barth, *Church Dogmatics* (T. & T. Clark), IV, 3 p. 498
3   Frederick Dale Bruner, *A Theology of the Holy Spirit* (Hodder & Stoughton), p. 168
4   John V. Taylor, *The Go-Between God* (S.C.M.), p. 112
5   Ibid. p. 202

CHAPTER THREE

Many Blessings—One Christ

FROM THE last chapter we have learnt that looking to Christ will, through faith and by the Spirit, produce in us an authentic reflection of his glory. A faith that does not begin to issue in experienced fulfilment in internal or external event falls far short of New Testament promise and expectation.

But now we have to insist with even greater vigour on the converse of that—religious experience has Christian relevance and validity, only when it has the marks of Christ upon it, and derives from him as its ultimate source, in some sense is a reflection of his own experience, and conforms to him and his word. We have already seen this Christocentric bias of the Spirit at work in the development of the New Testament doctrine of the Spirit, and also, as one example among many, in the present day charismatic renewal. Before we can proceed to examine it more closely, we must see what happens when the normative relationship between Christ and experience is not kept strictly and clearly in view.

The extreme case is when the relationship is completely reversed, and contemporary experience becomes the normative prototype, to which Christ and the gospel have to conform in order to find acceptance. I shall believe of Christ only what my human experience apart from Christ independently authenticates to me. The world that I know has no experience of New Testament miracles;

they are therefore unbelievable and have to be dismissed from the gospel, or reinterpreted in a way congenial to modern man. This is but an obvious example of the reductionist road that much Christian thinking has consistently trod in recent centuries. The gospel has had to be accommodated successively to the idealist mood of the nineteenth century and the existentialist mood of the twentieth, and in the process faith in all the essentials of the gospel, Trinity, incarnation, cross, resurrection and in scripture as their basis has been progressively eroded, so that they have all been deprived of their New Testament dimensions and forced into the framework of modern man's interpretation of his own experience. Christ is no longer the judge to whom every thought and feeling is subject; modern man has become the judge who adjudicates over him. This tendency appears in the most unexpected places, some of them very near to our own special concern.

We may ask, for instance, what is the root of the dispensationalism which has been the typical Protestant response to the New Testament descriptions of signs and wonders and charismatic gifts. Why do people try to make out that these were confined to the age of the apostles, till the canon of scripture was closed and the Church securely founded? Why does so biblically based a writer as John Stott, when he is dealing with the two lists of spiritual gifts in Romans 12 and 1 Corinthians 12, and discussing experiences of the Holy Spirit, repeatedly divide them into 'usual' and 'unusual', 'normal' and 'abnormal' gifts and experiences? (1) On what basis is this distinction made?

There is certainly no credible basis for it within the New Testament itself, which never distinguishes a set of experiences which are universally valid for all Christians in contrast with others which are dispensationally limited to the first Christians. For Paul 1 Corinthians 12 gifts and Romans 12 gifts are on the same footing, and distinctions between normal and abnormal, usual and unusual, natural and supernatural have been imposed upon them.

If we ask again, on what basis, the only answer is—on the basis of the historical and contemporary experience of the Church, in which some gifts have indeed been abnormal and unusual and often practically unknown. So, in the best manner of the Council of Trent, the tradition of the Church has been set up alongside scripture and has been allowed to control the interpretation of scripture. Because the Church has not for a long time experienced certain works of the Spirit, countless Christians have been told that they are 'not for now', so that they have had no expectation of faith towards certain biblical promises, and no openness to experience them. That is what happens when, even in the most self-consciously orthodox circles, religious experience seeks to conform the word to itself rather than to be open towards the word.

The same question about the relationship of our spiritual experience to its Christological norm arises in a way that is even more germane to our main enquiry, in connection with the 'second blessing' framework in which classical Pentecostalism, followed with different degrees of hesitation by many neo-Pentecostals, has presented its distinctive message about the baptism and gifts of the Holy Spirit.

It is not hard to see why this message should have been presented in this manner. In the first place, the early Pentecostalist movement was conditioned by its background in Methodist holiness teaching, to which the whole conception of two-stage Christianity was central. And even more importantly, people could claim that as a matter of personal testimony it had happened to them in this twofold way. They were converted Christians who had come to Christ and been justified by him, and now much later, in answer to faith and prayer, a second thing quite distinct from the first had happened to them—and they had entered into a new experience of the power, liberty and gifts of the Holy Spirit. And if what is at stake is simply a claim, as a matter of testimony, to have entered into such a distinctively new experience of a fresh dimension of the Spirit's work then many of us will gladly identify with their testimony, and say, "We were Christians before this came, but when it came, it marked a decisively new stage in our Christian life."

It is important to notice that it is one thing to testify to a new experience of the working of the Holy Spirit, and quite another to identify this experience as 'the second blessing'. The one is a description of what has happened, the other presupposes a particular theological interpretation of it. That you can have the experience, and yet not interpret it in this way, is something that the evangelical world in particular has found hard to grasp. Even the Church of Scotland Report, which recognises that Edward Irving interpreted the experience in a way that was Reformed-Calvinist rather than Methodist-holiness, yet betrays lingering suspicions that to claim any new experience of power at all is somehow inevitably to affirm the whole 'theology of subsequence', the whole second blessing view of it (2). That you can keep the experience and reject this theology is what we must try to show.

The testimony to the experience becomes a second blessing theology, when two things happen. First of all, you pass from factual description of how some people have in fact appropriated the blessings of the Spirit, to normative and universal statements about how everyone must enter these blessings, and you build on this a theological understanding of the relationship of Christ and the Spirit. In other words, on the basis of a valid testimony, there can be erected a law of spiritual experience, whereby the series 'conversion—fulfilment of certain conditions—baptism in the Spirit evidenced by speaking with tongues', can become the expected, prescribed and ultimately required progress of Christian experience. We can begin to say, "It happened to us this way, and it must happen to you this way also, because this is God's only way of making it happen, and if it does not happen this way, we shall not recognise its validity."

And, having set up this law, we can begin to theologise on the basis of it, and to suggest that there are two successive stages of Christian experience; a stage in which one receives Jesus and the blessings of forgiveness and reconciliation, which are the essential preconditions of all that is to follow; and a second stage at which one receives the Spirit and his power and gifts, and it is at this second stage that true spiritual effectiveness and satisfaction are to be found.

F. D. Bruner, by a careful selection of the most extreme statements he can find, tries to show that Pentecostalism has imprisoned itself in this theological straitjacket, and has then no difficulty in proving that the patient is, by New Testament standards, not of sound mind, and guilty of the Galatian aberration, the Colossian heresy, Corinthian gnosticism and much more besides.

It is very doubtful indeed if any Pentecostalist ever committed all the crimes that the pursuing Bruner alleges against him. Pentecostals have, in their actual practice, a far greater grasp of the centrality of Christ and his grace than Bruner is prepared to allow. It is one of their central affirmations that Jesus is the baptiser in the Holy Spirit, so that the whole realm of the Spirit and his gifts is in much more real subjection to the Lordship of Christ as its source, norm and end, than Bruner admits. Their statements are often much more spontaneous testimony than doctrinal teaching, and this has to be remembered in our estimation of them.

But nevertheless, however unjust he may have been to the reality of living Pentecostalism, Bruner puts us in his debt for quite relentlessly drawing out the implications of the second blessing presentation of the work of the Holy Spirit, for exposing its inability to present what the New Testament actually says about Christ and the Spirit, and its dangerous tendencies to obscure and deny some central New Testament teaching. This is entirely helpful, because it is not too much to say that many Christians find it hard to hear the necessary things that Pentecostals are saying to the churches, precisely because of their unhappiness and perplexities about the 'two-stage' framework in which it is set. There are two main areas of this perplexity which we may discuss in turn.

1   Is there in fact a law of spiritual experience in the New Testament—one prescribed way of coming step by step into God's blessings, first in Christ and then in the Holy Spirit?

A lady in Belfast once focussed these perplexities for me by asking, "How many blessings are there? The Baptists say you get everything when you are converted, the Faith Mission say there is a second blessing for total sanctification, the Pentecostals say there is a blessing of the Spirit that gives power for service. How many blessings are there?" One might rather naughtily quote the hymnwriter in a sense he never intended "Count your many blessings, name them one by one, and it will surprise you what the Lord has done!"

We may well ask whether we are meant to use our personal experience of Christ and his grace to make universal laws of this kind. I can find in the New Testament no positive suggestion that the Spirit comes to people in some set order of experiences and gifts. In particular there is just no trace in the New Testament of a universal law of Christian progress that lays down that we must first be converted and then, after an interval, go on to be baptised in the Spirit. The New Testament assumption is that all Christians are in the full experiential flow of the Spirit's life and power, because in being initiated into Christ they have come to know the full release of the Spirit as well. In Samaria and at Ephesus, there were believers for whom this was not so, but far from being typical, they were the subnormal exceptions with whom urgent measures had to be taken to bring them up to spiritual par, which means not to some second experience beyond Christ, but to appropriation of all that has already been offered them in him.

The accounts in Acts of the coming of the Holy Spirit upon different groups of Christians show that there is no monotonous uniformity but rather a glorious variety in the human experiences involved. He came spontaneously to the apostles at Pentecost, and we are even told in Acts 4:31 that he came to the same people a second time, so that, as John Taylor comments (3), even the conferring of second blessings is not excluded from his repertoire. He came to the Samaritans when apostolic hands were laid upon them, to Paul when he was being healed by the unapostolic hands of Ananias, to Cornelius as the gospel was preached, to the Ephesian disciples when hands were laid upon them in the context of their baptism in water.

We may take any of these incidents and find that its main features are paralleled in contemporary experience, but we may turn none of them into rule or rubric. To quote John Taylor again, "The Holy Spirit does not appear to have read the rubrics! He will not and cannot be bound." (4)

To be even more specific, there is no law of tongues in the New Testament. The legalistic assertion of some Pentecostals that an authentic experience of the baptism in the Spirit must be accompanied by speaking in tongues as its initial evidence, goes beyond any scriptural statement. By the grace of God to speak in tongues is the first new gift of the Spirit conferred on some Christians when they are filled with the Spirit, but this has to do rather with God's gracious response to the needs of their personality than the fulfilment of some legal requirement, and the concentration upon and demand for tongues that result from the imposition of such a requirement lead to the most unfortunate pastoral consequences.

The Holy Spirit is indeed always doing the same things, but he is always doing them differently, in an endless creativity that has no need to repeat itself. The norm for the working of the Spirit that we are seeking is not to be found in the shape of the experience itself, and we can do untold harm to people by telling them they have to be converted in a certain way or baptised in the Spirit in a certain way. To try to impose such a law of spiritual experience upon the gospel is in the end of the day to make a universal norm out of sheer subjectivism, to turn our eyes, when we are looking for standards, upon ourselves and our experiences and to demand that others repeat them; instead of looking to Christ.

2   But the situation becomes even more difficult when the two-stage theory of our reception of the Spirit is made not only a law for others, but turned into a theology that claims to explain the action of God, so that we assert not only that we come to Christian completeness through two distinct experiences, but that God him-

self is offering us two distinct gifts, first salvation and justification in Christ, and then a receiving of the Holy Spirit which adds what was lacking in the first.

Such a presentation is significantly different from the New Testament in the following ways:

(a) It obscures the unity of the gospel. There are now two segregated areas of divine giving; over the first Christ crucified presides and the Holy Spirit has a mediatorial work of bringing Christ to us and us to him. In the second the Holy Spirit himself is central and the function of Christ is to bring the Spirit to us to do his own distinctive work. Christ and the Spirit are operative in both areas, but they almost exchange functions. In the first Christ is Lord and the Spirit his servant, in the second the Spirit is Lord and Christ his servant. This is precisely the situation described in the Pentecostalist teaching of Ralph M. Riggs, "As the Spirit of Christ, he had come at conversion, imparting the Christ-life, revealing Christ and making him real. At the baptism in the Spirit, he himself in his own person comes upon and fills the waiting believer. This experience is as distinct from conversion as the Holy Spirit is distinct from Christ. His coming to the believer at the baptism [in the Holy Spirit] is the coming of the Third Person of the Trinity, in addition to the coming of Christ which takes place at conversion." (5)

Such a statement may indeed reduce us to theological tears. Only part of our Christian experience is related to Christ, the remainder and the best part of it is experience of the Spirit. The unity of the gospel is here called radically into question. From this there follows another even more devastating consequence:

(b) The second blessing presentation obscures the centrality and sufficiency of the Lord Jesus Christ. He becomes the Lord of the beginning, of the so-far; but at a decisive point he hands us over to the Holy Spirit who is Lord of the 'further' and the 'more'. The great reluctance of many good Christian people to go on listening at this point is very understandable. Here indeed is a second gospel of the Holy Spirit being so preached as to challenge the sole Lordship of Christ, that offers to lead us past him into something that is beyond him and better than him, into a world of sensational experiences and gifts which may satisfy our religious cravings but are in very uncertain and ambiguous relationship to the gospel of Christ, incarnate, crucified, risen and coming. In face of that, people who say that they will not take one step beyond Christ may well have our sympathy.

For if we return to the question we asked earlier, "How many blessings are there?" the New Testament answer is "essentially one!" God has given us his one gift of himself in his Son, and everything else is contained in him. "Blessed be the God and Father of our Lord Jesus Christ, who has blessed us *in Christ with every spiritual blessing* in the heavenly places" (Eph. 1:3). However many and varied our spiritual experiences, they all have their unity and significance in the fact that they all proceed from him, reflect him and glorify him. He is the centre and unity of all that comes to us from God, and anything that does not derive ultimately from that centre, whatever its experiential quality, is without Christian value or context.

Any suggestion that some of the blessing and some of the fullness have their residence in Christ and that the 'more' has its residence elsewhere, is not only not supported, but explicitly denied in the New Testament. "In him the whole fulness of deity dwells bodily, and you have come to fulness of life in him" (Col. 2:9–10), and therefore we are not to explore in other spiritual directions so that we "lose hold upon the Head; yet it is from the Head that the whole body, with all its joints and ligaments receives its supplies, and thus knit together, grows according to God's design" (Col. 2:19). According to John 1:16 there is to be received from Christ "grace upon grace", one gracious gift piled on another, and we are to explore the richness of it in every glorious dimension. But the place from which we are to receive is "from his fulness" (*ek tou pleromatos autou*) and nowhere else at all.

All this is of course known and affirmed by Pentecostals as much as by anybody else, but the whole second blessing statement of the matter, draws us relentlessly away from the Christian centre, and makes us glorify the Spirit, when we are specifically told that it is the business of the Spirit to glorify Christ. There is no answer to the question which the Church of Scotland Report asks at this point, "How can faith in Christ, the sole Lord and Saviour of men, the only King and Head of the Church, be a half-way house where the believer receives life, but not sufficient power to witness and to serve?" (6)

It must indeed be a faith that is open to all that is in Christ, whose face really is unveiled to all the glory of the Lord, but it must and need not search for anything that it needs anywhere else but in him. There is more in him than any of us have yet realised, but it is all in him.

(c) The second blessing presentation obscures the function of the Holy Spirit. According to it, in the application of salvation the Holy Spirit takes from Christ and gives to us, but in the realm of baptism in the Spirit, the Holy Spirit does his own thing, his own independent work as the "third person of the Holy Trinity". The Spirit belongs to both realms but he functions differently in each, in one he brings what is Christ's, in the other what is his own.

To set this right we have only to quote again the key verse John 16:14–15, "He will glorify me, for he will take what is mine and declare it to you. All that the Father has is mine." The Holy Spirit in every aspect of his activity is the Spirit of Christ; when he comes, Christ comes, to be in Christ is to be in the Spirit (Rom. 8:9, 10, 11). In the triune Godhead there is oneness of being, but subordination of function. The Son says and does nothing that he does not receive from the Father, the Spirit gives nothing he has not received from the Son. In the Son the glory of the Father becomes incarnate among us, in the Spirit that same glory becomes experiential within us.

Thus there is no divide between Son and Spirit. The power

that came upon the Church at Pentecost was the same power that first came upon Jesus in Jordan, there is nothing working in us that did not first work in him. The chief agent in the gospel narratives is the Son of God operating in and through the humanity he has taken to himself in the power of his Spirit: in Acts the same agent is working by the same Spirit in and through the men he has called to himself. The cross does not operate only in the preliminary stages of the Christian life, so that we can leave it behind, and proceed into some realm of Christian triumphalism, the Spirit and the cross belong together all the way. None of the works or gifts or fruit of the Spirit have any importance in and for themselves, but only in so far as they glorify Christ's name and further Christ's mission and edify Christ's Body.

The Spirit is known by the fact that where he is at work there is confession of Christ and conformity to Christ, "By this you know the Spirit of God; every spirit which confesses that Jesus Christ has come in the flesh is of God, and every spirit which does not confess Jesus is not of God" (1 John 4:2-3). The pattern of the Spirit's life is the pattern of Christ's life, "By this we know that we abide in him, and he in us, because he has given us of his own Spirit (*ek tou pneumatos autou*)" (John 4:13).

The Holy Spirit is not honoured by being set in some imagined competition with or superiority over the Lord Jesus Christ. It is an honour he declines, because his work is to lead us past himself, so that in every experience he brings us we confess "Jesus is Lord".

(d) The second blessing presentation can obscure the sovereignty of grace. If asked why everyone who comes to Christ does not experience immediately the fullness of the Spirit, some, not all, proponents of this view will reply that it is because the human conditions have not been fulfilled; there has not been a radical enough repentance, or a deep enough faith, or a fervent enough prayer, or a complete enough consecration. The blessing of the Spirit is thus thought of as being granted in response to

moral and spiritual attainments. We are told that the Holy
Spirit cannot dwell in an unclean heart, which implies that
cleanness of heart is to be attained as a prior condition for the
indwelling of the Spirit, rather than as a result of that indwelling.

All this removes Spirit-baptism on to a completely different
basis from salvation in Christ, which is by grace alone and
through faith alone, "By grace you have been saved through
faith; and this is not your own doing, it is the gift of God—not
because of works lest any man should boast" (Eph. 2:8-9). We
must be quite clear that according to the New Testament the
Holy Spirit, like the whole gift of salvation in Christ, of which
he is a part, is given entirely on the ground of Christ's sacrifice
for us, and not of any attainment of our own. All his operations
are charismatic—that is, they are the operation of undeserved
grace. Even the carnal Corinthians could receive genuine gifts
of the Spirit. The state of their sanctification affected the way
they handled them, but was obviously not a prior condition of
their being conferred.

The conclusive statement here is in Acts 2:38, "Repent and
be baptised, every one of you in the name of Jesus Christ for the
forgiveness of your sins and you shall receive the gift of the Holy
Spirit." Here the gift of the Spirit, in all its Pentecostal fullness,
as the crowd had seen it that day conferred on the apostles, is
offered to the same people and on the same conditions as forgiveness in Christ. Here indeed the only condition is repentance,
understood not as some meritorious work which has power in
itself to attract or earn the promised blessing, but as a turning
from ourselves and all our works to Christ and all his promises,
as the means by which his gift of forgiveness and the Spirit may
come to us.

All second blessing teaching whether of a Pentecostal or
'holiness' type, is in danger of dividing the Christian life into a
salvation which is gift to the sinner, and the fullness of the
Spirit which is reward of the saint, and thus maligning the central

gospel principle that from beginning to end is all of grace. The feeling of not being good enough is a frequent practical hindrance to those seeking the release of the Spirit, and the only answer is that this is a free gift of the Father, available on the basis of the Son's work and intercession, by grace alone.

(e) The second blessing presentation obscures the unity of God's people. It provides theological justification for a division of Christians into two classes, those who have 'only received Jesus' and those who have gone on to 'receive the Spirit' as well: those who have fulfilled certain conditions and so attained superior blessings, and those who have not. Such absolute distinctions lay the foundation for that divisive élitism which can be the curse of revivalism, and which the present charismatic renewal has also known.

There are obviously endless differences in maturity and effectiveness among Christians, but they are not differences of this kind. All of Christ and all of the Spirit is offered to all Christians, and withheld from none, as the great gift of God's grace, and the differences arise not between 'haves' and 'have-nots' in regard to the Spirit, but solely from the degree to which Christians have entered into enjoyment of the inheritance that belongs to all of them and possessed the possessions that are for all in Christ. The charismatics dare not claim to be exclusively charismatic, but simply to remind the Church of the neglected charismatic element that is at the basis of its life. D. T. Niles once defined evangelism as one beggar telling another where to find bread. Pentecostal renewal can only be the same beggar telling his brother that in the same place where there is bread, there is living water also.

For all these reasons we have to reject a 'second blessing' interpretation of the work of the Spirit. It starts, not from a norm in Christ and scripture, but from a norm in experience, which it erects into a law and a doctrine which does serious despite to the gospel and to Christ's place as the one centre of the gospel. Our entrance into our inheritance may have been by two crisis experiences—just as it may have been in some quite different way—but to understand the significance of our experience, we are not to look at its form, but rather at Christ as its source, norm and end. Experience is to be explained in terms of Christ, not Christ in terms of experience. The experience is but a reflection of the original, who is Jesus, and is to find its explanation in him.

The question immediately arises as to how positively we have to understand the Pentecostal experience if we reject the second blessing interpretation of it, which has been its usual context. The Church of Scotland Report goes so far as to recommend that we abandon the whole 'baptism in the Spirit' terminology, on the ground that it is so completely tainted with the theology of subsequence as to be untenable where that theology is rejected.

In this we do not propose to follow the Church of Scotland; I shall maintain that baptism in the Spirit is one legitimate way of describing what is an integral part of the gift of Christ. But in faithfulness to the principle we have laid down, we are not in a position to discuss that directly at this point. In order to understand the reflected work of the Spirit in us, we first have to understand the original work of the Spirit in Christ, and the positive understanding of the Pentecostal experience must wait until we can return to it with that prior task fulfilled.

Notes to Chapter Three

NOTES

1   John R. W. Stott, *The Baptism and Fullness of the Holy Spirit* (I.V.F.), pp. 36–40.

2   cf "Some members of the working party questioned this stress on power, which they felt was the result of the theology of

subsequence" *The Charismatic Movement in the Church of Scotland* p. 14

3 John V. Taylor, *The Go-Between God* (S.C.M.), p. 119

4 Ibid. p. 120

5 Ralph M. Riggs, *The Spirit Himself* (Springfield Mo., Gospel Publishing House), pp. 79–80 (quoted by F. D. Bruner op. cit. p. 71)

6 *The Charismatic Movement in the Church of Scotland* p. 5

CHAPTER FOUR

Christ's Earthly Glory

WE HAVE now to look more closely at the relationship between Christ and Spirit which we have seen to be central in New Testament teaching. Essentially it consists of what Professor T. F Torrance describes as a double mediation, "In his new coming the Holy Spirit is mediated by Christ, and at the same time mediates Christ to us." (1)

So, on the one hand (a) the Spirit is mediated by Christ, not merely in the sense that Christ sends the Spirit, but in the stronger sense that the work which the Holy Spirit does in us is totally determined by the work that he has first done in Christ. Jesus is the original prototype of the spiritual man, and everything that happens in us by the Spirit is reflection of what has happened in him. Our main task in succeeding chapters is to discover in detail what this means.

But, first, let us look at the other side of the coin and see (b) that the Spirit mediates Christ to us. Following upon the work that the Spirit does *in* Christ *for* us, there is the work that he does *in* us *for* Christ. Not only does the Spirit depend upon Christ for the original he wants to reproduce in us, but Christ depends upon the work of the Spirit in order that what he has done for us may not remain ineffective, but may be revealed and set into activity among us.

In its Godward aspect, the work of Christ is completed; its result is the exaltation of Jesus as Lord. God has given him the name that is above every name and all power at his right hand (Phil. 2:9–11), so that his heavenly glory is secure. But on earth every knee has not yet bowed nor every tongue confessed. He has from his ascension a heavenly glory with his Father, but he has still to find an earthly glory in his Church, a manifestation on earth of his risen rule and presence.

Pentecost marks his entry into this earthly glory; the Spirit whom he has sent begins to mediate the Lord to men in all his power, his kingdom takes its first step towards coming on earth as it has already come in heaven.

A favourite New Testament way, especially in Acts, of expressing this mediating ministry of the Holy Spirit is to speak of his being Christ's witness, who by his operation in others makes them also witnesses. Acts 1:8 expresses the whole purpose of receiving power (*dunamis*) from on high as being "you shall be my witnesses" (*esesthe mou martureis*). But Acts 5:32 makes it clear that the coming of the Holy Spirit constitutes us as Christ's witnesses, only because he himself is pre-eminently *the* Witness to Christ. Having recounted the main gospel essentials Peter says, "and we are witnesses to these things, and so is the Holy Spirit, whom God has given".

A witness is qualified as such by his first hand participation in the events he attests, and his function is to come forward in a new situation, where these events are being examined, in order that by authority of his first-hand knowledge he may win a verdict of acceptance for what he represents. As distinct from a witness in a lawcourt, the important thing about the New Testament witness is not simply the testimony that he gives. The Holy Spirit does not promise to give us power merely to bear testimony, but to *be* witnesses. The whole life and being of the Christian community, and not simply those activities which it undertakes with a specifically evangelistic intention, constitute its witness to Christ. By the Spirit the Christian knows Christ and participates in Christ, so that in all that he is and does, in his relationships with his Father and his brethren, the reality of Christ keeps coming through.

It is the whole work of the Holy Spirit to give us that shared life (*koinonia*) with Christ that will entitle and enable us to be his witnesses. He is qualified to do that, because he is himself the great Witness, who was in the making of that to which he witnesses, in the birth, baptism, ministry, dying, rising and ascending of the one to whom he testifies.

To communicate Christ to us so that we may communicate him to others is the unifying purpose in all the various operations of the Spirit. So he *illuminates* us, through the apostolic witness of scripture, often mediated through the contemporary witness of the Church, into a spiritual knowledge of Christ, so that the whole reality of the living Christ and his work is opened to us. "So also no one comprehends the thoughts of God except the Spirit of God. Now we have received not the Spirit of the world, but the Spirit which is from God, that we might understand the gifts bestowed on us by God" (1 Cor. 2:11-12).

But we can never, as Calvin said, know the Lord in his glory without at the same time coming to see ourselves in our misery. Thus the illuminating work of the Spirit inevitably implies his *convicting* work in which, by showing us Christ and his grace, he shows us also ourselves and our need, "When he comes he will convince the world of sin, of righteousness and of judgment" (John 16:8).

But this illumination and conviction further implies *regeneration*. The seeing of the rule of God, which is the same as entering the kingdom of God, is not a natural possibility for any of us; it involves our remaking at depth, our rebirth and re-creation by the operation of the Spirit upon us, so that we can enter into a new set of relationships with God and his people. "Unless a man is born again of water and the Spirit, he cannot see or enter the kingdom of God" (John 3:5 cf 3:3).

And the Spirit reveals to us the status into which we have been so born, and does in us a work óf *assurance*, "When we cry Abba, Father it is the Spirit bearing witness with our spirits that we are children of God, and if children, then heirs, joint heirs with Christ" (Rom. 8:15-17). The Spirit tells us who we are and gives us confidence as sons of the Father and co-heirs with Christ to claim in faith our joint inheritance.

Thus the Spirit begins to shape us into the likeness of Christ, in three different ways. First, he catches us up into that relationship that Christ has with his Father, and so performs his work as *Paraclete* or Intercessor. Christ is interceding high priest at the Father's right hand, and the Spirit identifies us with him in his intercession, "Likewise the Spirit helps us in our weakness, for we do not know how to pray as we ought, but the Spirit himself intercedes for us with sighs too deep for words. And he who searches the hearts of men knows what is the mind of the Spirit, because the Spirit intercedes for the saints according to the will of God" (Rom. 8:26-27).

And as we are brought into the likeness of Christ's prayer, so we are brought into the likeness of Christ's character. The Spirit sets himself against our fallen flesh and its desires, so that the fruit of the Spirit (Gal. 5:22) which is the likeness of Christ is formed and matured in us, and so we are *sanctified.*

But the likeness of Christ is also the likeness of one who is "mighty in deed and word before God and all the people" (Luke 24:19), so that there is an *empowering* work of the Spirit, by which the works that he did we do also and greater works than these, now that he has gone to the Father (John 14:12). His power is no less available to us than his love; his gifts can operate as surely as his fruits can grow, because by both we are brought into related but distinct aspects of his likeness.

We have recapitulated briefly the main things that scripture has to say about the work of the Spirit in order that we may see them in their unity. For it is this illuminated, convicted, regenerated man, reinstated in his sonship, participating in Christ's life, his prayer, his character and power, who, when he is joined by the same Spirit into one Body with others like him, can be the qualified witness to Jesus Christ in the world.

These things are done in us, not just for our personal salvation, which in the New Testament is never seen as an end in itself, but in order that the present, living glory of Christ may be manifested among us in word and action and relationship. Our regeneration, sanctification and empowering are not for ourselves, to be hidden away in the secret of our hearts or behind the closed doors of our small fellowship. They are given to qualify us as witnesses who will assert our witness in all sorts of new situations and so reveal Christ there.

In Acts 2 the phenomena of Pentecost are never allowed to become an independent source of interest. They serve in the first place the preliminary task of gathering a crowd for Peter's sermon, and then they serve as supporting evidence for its main theme. That theme is not the events of that morning in the upper room. Peter does not dwell on the sensational transformation through which he and his friends have passed. He says what needs to be said about the tongues, and passes on quickly to the proclamation of the crucified, risen and ascended Lord.

And yet in doing so he by no means leaves the phenomena of Pentecost out of account. The Jesus of whom he is speaking is defined as the one who is so real and living, that he has provided in his servants and by his Spirit audible and visible witness—not just the tongues, but these transformed men speaking in tongues and proclaiming his Gospel—as first hand evidence that he is Lord, "He has poured out this which you see and hear" (Acts 2:33). Because of what can be seen and heard his resurrected rule is brought out of the realm of verbal assertion, and shown to be of such relevance and consequence here and now, that it urgently requires those to whom it is communicated to declare their attitude to it.

Here indeed is a picture of what it is to be a witness under the inspiration of the great Witness. A deep personal work is done in Christ's servants so that their lives are in a new way joined with his life, and that breaks out into words and deeds and a shared life that proclaim the Lord's presence. He is shut up neither in history nor in heaven, but he is here and now. And here and now he operates, not only in the hidden awareness of the soul, as a still small voice or a gracious influence—although all that is also within his province—but he manifests himself, as he did in the days of his flesh, by the lives that he transformingly touches, the authoritative words that he speaks, and the mighty deeds that he performs, so that the lineaments of his love and the operations of his power begin to appear among his people.

The characteristic Christian slogan of our time, declares "Jesus is alive today", and the manifestations of his Spirit are the evidences and signs that this is so. Christ is dependent on this witness of the Spirit for the full manifestation of his glory here on earth, and where the work of the Spirit is inhibited or frustrated, there the glory of Christ is abbreviated and restricted.

It is failure to grasp the element of witness to a living Christ as quite central to the New Testament presentation of the work of the Spirit which has led many traditional writers on the person and work of the Spirit, first to dispensationalise, and then largely to ignore the specifically charismatic element in the New Testament—i.e. that part which has to do with the manifestation of the Lord's presence openly among his people. For such writers the whole centre of concern is human salvation, conceived of in a mainly inward and religious way, so that the outward manifestations of power seem irrelevant and crude intrusions into the delicate dealings between the Lord and the souls he is saving. That is why in such works as George Smeaton's *The Doctrine of the Holy Spirit* and James Buchanan's *The Office and Work of the Holy Spirit* and in much popular evangelicalism there is an almost exclusive concentration on the beginning of the Christian life in the Spirit's work in regeneration. The whole thrust of God's purpose in Christ as executed by the Spirit is to bring men to reconciliation and relationship with God, so that in comparison even moral sanctification becomes a quite subsidiary interest.

But the whole perspective changes if we ask, as Karl Barth asked most impressively in the final complete volume of his *Church Dogmatics* (IV, 3), "For what purpose are men saved and brought to God?" and if we accept Barth's interpretation of the New Testament answer, "In order that they may reveal his kingdom in its nearness and presence and by the witnesses of his Lordship over every area of human life." The New Testament has less interest in the saved individual in and for himself than some of our traditions have led us to suppose. The end of God's action is the revelation of God's kingdom and glory rather than simply the personal impartation of salvation. To grasp that gives the outward manifestations of the Spirit, his gifting of Christ's Body and his joining of Christ's members into a visible community of corporate living, a new importance and centrality. We can see now why the Holy Spirit cannot stay hidden in the heart, why he has to break out from the upper room into the open forum, and in the combined witness of his people's life, deed, and word proclaim where the world can see and hear that Jesus is Lord.

The signs of Christ's kingdom need to be given not only in inner transformations in the soul, but in acts of power in the physical and psychological spheres and, especially, in concrete form in the life of the local body which he calls to represent him—so that everywhere evidence may be given of the Lord's reign.

Where the great Witness is not released in this way to make us Christ's witnesses, then inevitably Christ withdraws into remoteness, and is robbed of his earthly glory and the Church withdraws into its own religious self-concern. It is significant that at a time when contemporary society is increasingly fascinated with the figure of Christ and buys endless books about him, it has nothing but disregard for the in-concerns of the churches, the historical research, and doctrinal argument, and ecclesiastical rearrangements, that so absorb churchmen. A Christ who is distant in history, or remote in heaven, or coming in some indefinitely delayed future, imprisoned in all our complicated verbal formulae encapsulated in liturgical form in service or sacrament, or in pious form in the hidden inwardness of the heart, has little appeal for our kind of world.

Only when the Holy Spirit moves, and the whole range of New Testament things start happening and the Church is gathered and shaped visibly into the community of his Body, does the Church begin to function relevantly and effectively, so that Christ and the claims that we make for him become real issues for people. The healing of a little girl in the name of Jesus can say to a whole watching street of neighbours that Jesus is Lord—in a way that all the words spoken in the Church, at which most of them are never present, can quite fail to do. The Lord Jesus has walked out of the religious in-world and come down our street; the kingdom has again drawn near and shown itself to be among us, and it becomes in a new way an urgent question for us what we shall do with the King.

So the Spirit mediates the Son and gives him his earthly glory. It is in a context of Pentecostal manifestation, rather than of theological enquiry, that Peter makes his final climactic statement —and it is the manifestation which provides the evidence for the truth of what he says, "Let all the house of Israel know assuredly that God has made this Jesus, whom you crucified, both Lord and Christ" (Acts 2:36).

The specific witness of the events of Pentecost is that Jesus is the Christ. He is not only Jesus, who saves his people from their sins (Matthew 1:21), and not only Lord, *Kurios*, exalted to the right hand of the Father and given a name which is above every name (Phil. 2:9), but he is also *Christos*, Messiah, the King of Israel anointed with divine power, and calling others into his messianic company to share the same anointing and to be *Christ*-ians. He who was anointed with the Holy Spirit and with power (Acts 10:38) in his own baptism in Jordan is, in virtue of his death and resurrection, the one who anoints his people with the same Holy Spirit and the same power at Pentecost. The function of the charismatic renewal is basically, put in Christological terms, to remind the Church that Jesus is also the Christ; the one who was crucified for sin is also the one who pours out his Spirit to make us credible witnesses to his inaugurated, but still to be completed kingdom.

It is important that we should see his two titles in both their distinctness and their unity. There is no Christ who is not also Jesus, there is no outpouring of the Spirit which is not the consequence of the offering once made on the cross. Fears that a gospel of the baptiser in the Spirit might replace the gospel of the crucified Saviour, and we might escape from repentance into a spurious triumphalism of spiritual experiences and gifts, are real fears. The spirit-filled life has no foundation when it does not spring from a reckoning with the cross. I would have to confess that in early days of charismatic enthusiasm I ministered to people regarding the outpouring of the Spirit, without having made sufficient enquiry about the soundness of their Christian foundations, and lived to regret it when I saw what uncrucified carnality could do to spiritual experience. It is of the utmost theological and pastoral importance, to establish more precisely the connection between the work of Calvary and the gift of Pentecost. Paul puts it memorably to the Ephesians, when, commenting on Psalm 68:18 he says, "In saying he ascended what does it mean but that he had also descended into the lower parts of the earth." (Eph. 4:9) The gospel of the ascended Lord who pours out his gifts is also the gospel of the humiliated Servant who pours out his blood.

But Paul also says, "He who descended is also he who ascended far above all the heavens, that he might fill all things. And his gifts were . . ." (Eph. 4:10, 11). We are not so to concentrate our attention and our faith on the Saviour who pardons that we allow the Christ who anoints and gives his gifts to fall into the background. Sometimes Jesus has been presented as forgiving the sins of yesterday and opening the kingdom of heaven tomorrow by his blood and grace, but as having somehow departed into heaven and left today to us. We have been saved in the power of his blood, but have to live the Christian life out of the resources of our own humanity, by pious dedication and consecration, or by organised religions, evangelistic or social activism—so that instead of the principle of grace covering the whole of our life, we behave as if we had been saved by grace, but have to live by our own works. A gospel that over-concentrates on a Jesus who forgives, and forgets that his ministry as the crucified has its essential sequel in his continuing work in providing for the whole activity of his people out of his own resources and by the gifts of his Spirit, can easily fall foul of Paul's question to the Galatians, "Having begun in the Spirit, are you ending with the flesh?" (Gal. 3:3) Pentecost proclaims that God's work is only and always done in the energy of Christ's Spirit, that the grace (*charis*) that saves us goes on becoming concrete in the gifts (*charismata*) he bestows. A crucified Jesus who is not also an anointed Christ is but abstraction from the wholeness of the gospel. That abstraction has sometimes been offered almost as though it was the whole, so that his Christ-function has been obscured and not been properly offered to or appropriated by our faith, and so has not appeared with its New Testament decisiveness in the life of the Church.

The offer that Peter makes is a full offer, because the Christ he has proclaimed is a full Christ. "Repent and be baptised every one of you for the forgiveness of your sins and you shall receive the gift of the Holy Spirit." (Acts 2:38) Baptismal initiation into the Lord in the full New Testament understanding of it, is a turning round (repentance) to Jesus who is also Christ, so that the Jesus-factor—forgiveness, and the Christ-factor—the gift of the Spirit, are both imparted to the believer.

So the Spirit himself witnesses, and makes us witness, to the Jesus who is the Christ, who in his one grace has given himself to us, in order to establish his earthly glory among us.

Notes to Chapter Four

NOTE

1   T. F. Torrance, *Theology in Reconstruction* (S.C.M.), p. 245

CHAPTER FIVE

Behold the Man!

WE HAVE identified what could be called the mutual mediation of
Christ and Spirit, whereby, on the one hand, it is the Spirit who
brings us Christ, and, on the other, it is Christ who brings us the
Spirit. We have seen in the last chapter something of how the
Spirit brings us Christ, and have now to see how Christ mediates
the Spirit to us. We are now approaching the very centre of our
concern, and the Christological heart of everything that we have
to say about the Holy Spirit. In speaking about the part of the
Spirit in the being and mission of Jesus, we are treading on the
holiest of holy ground.

In this chapter we shall try to construct the outlines of a
Christological framework for the Spirit's work, and in following
chapters, as we look at the place of the Spirit in the gospel history
of Jesus, we shall try to see in greater detail how all the pieces are
held together within that frame.

Proceeding first in the most general terms, we discover that the
relationship of the Holy Spirit to the Lord Jesus Christ has again
a twofold nature. F. J. Leenhardt, commenting on Romans 1:4,
says, "The Son is at once the Bearer and Dispenser of the Spirit"
(1); he receives the Spirit and he bestows the Spirit.

This is clearly illustrated in the gospel accounts of the baptism
of Jesus by John. On the one hand the Spirit comes down upon

him as he emerges from the baptismal waters. As Peter later comments, "God anointed Jesus of Nazareth with the Holy Spirit and with power" (Acts 10:38), so that he becomes the Bearer of the Spirit. But on the other hand it is central to the prophecy of the Baptist that the coming one's great mission, alongside that of being the lamb of God who takes away the sin of the world, is to confer the Holy Spirit. "He will baptise you with the Holy Spirit and with fire" (Luke 3:16). He stands humbly in Jordan to receive the power which one day he will in kingly majesty bestow upon his people. John precisely repeats the same double emphasis at this point, "He who sent me to baptise with water said to me, 'He on whom you see the Spirit descend and remain, this is he who baptises with the Holy Spirit'" (John 1:33). We have to bear both these aspects of his relationship to the Spirit equally in mind, if we are going to describe it adequately. We look now at each in turn.

1   He is the *Receiver* of the Spirit, the original prototype to whom the Father has given the Spirit without measure (John 3:34). He is the original and we are the copy, but we must ask, "On what basis can we be like him? If the Spirit is able to reflect in us what he did in him, what is the common factor between us, the basic stuff that the Spirit can in each case mould and form into the same shape? As we look at Christ and see all that makes him different from us, what do we see in him that he shares with us, and that can serve as a basis for our being changed into his likeness?"

The answer is that the common factor is our manhood which he shares. In both Christ and us the Spirit is working with the stuff of our common humanity; because he is man and we are men, it becomes possible and credible that what the Spirit did first in him, he should be able to do again in us. "The Word became flesh and dwelt among us and we beheld his glory" (John 1:14). The glory of the Lord has shone, not in the disincarnate divinity of the eternal Word, where it could only dazzle or appal us, but in the flesh of the man Jesus, which the Word has taken to itself. What we see when we look at Jesus Christ is the Man; a work has been done in the midst of humanity, the very humanity that constitutes my being—which is the new standard for, and promise to all men.

And this is a work of the Holy Spirit. Jesus's humanity has its origin in his conception by the Holy Spirit; it has its effectiveness from its anointing by the Holy Spirit. This new man, Jesus Christ, is the work of the Son of God operating in his own human nature in the power and energy of the Holy Spirit. Therefore, seeing what the Spirit can do and has done in his flesh, we have a picture and a promise of what he can do in ours. Paul tells the Ephesians that the work of Christ in the Church goes on "until we all attain ... to mature manhood, to the measure of the stature of the fullness of Christ" (Eph. 4:13). The fullness of Christ can almost be equated with mature manhood, because the fullness of the Godhead has dwelt in Christ bodily, *somatikos*, in human form (Col. 2:9).

From this general Christological starting point several vital implications emerge:

(a) God always works *incarnationally*. There could be no more vital and liberating insight for those seeking renewal by the Holy Spirit, than to take with practical seriousness the fact that the raw material of the work of the Holy Spirit is our humanity, and all that he does is in and for our manhood, first in Jesus and then in us.

It is no accident that 1 John 4 makes the sign of the genuineness of spiritual utterances, not just the confession that Jesus Christ has come—but that he has come *in the flesh*—(1 John 4:2), that the abundant creativity of God has expressed itself in human form as the first fruits of a new humanity, and that everything that expresses and enhances that new humanity has the mark of the Holy Spirit upon it, and everything that suppresses and distorts that humanity or denies it its wholeness is *ipso facto* not of the Holy Spirit, however ecstatic or 'spiritual' or charismatic it may appear.

Alongside a theological docetism which refuses to take

seriously the humanity of the unique Son of God, there is a practical docetism which refuses to take seriously the humanity of the adopted children of God, which despises the outward body and cultivates the inner spirit with a wrong exclusiveness, which regards the created flesh with suspicion and the realm of religion as co-extensive with the Kingdom of God, which depreciates the natural gifts of creation, in favour of the 'supernatural' gifts of grace, and does not see that the absolute opposition that it sets up between them is quite unscriptural.

God expressed himself and his grace in Christ not *ecstatically* —that is by taking us out of our humanity, by dealing with us apart from what he had created us to be, cancelling out nature by supernature—but *incarnationally*, by taking our humanity out of its alienation and self-sufficiency and opening it up to himself, so that all its suppressed and distorted potentialities are released by the creativity of the Holy Spirit, and used to compose the likeness of Christ. Grace perfects creation and does not abolish it (as Aquinas nearly said); it brings creation back to the point where it finds the wholeness, that it does not have in itself, in the re-establishment of its *koinonia*, its shared life with God. The Holy Spirit is the Spirit of Jesus, and he comes to us clothed in Christ's humanity, not to make us super-spiritual saints, or ascetic anchorites, or miracle-mongering supernaturalists, or chandelier-swinging fanatics—but quite simply to make us men.

(b) We are putting the same point only slightly differently when we say that the concern of Jesus is for the *wholeness* of our humanity. The Spirit of the Lord is upon him and has anointed him so that he may release men and make them whole. (Luke 4:18) The effect of the release of the Spirit in a friend of mine was later described (by his wife!) as having made him "far less religious and far more normal".

If it did that it was indeed a work of the Holy Spirit, for according to *Today's English Version of the New Testament*, God's "Spirit fills us with power and love and self-control"

(II Tim 1:7). The Greek of the last word is *sophronismos*, which A.V. renders 'sound mind', but which could almost be rendered 'balanced normality', and the verse emphasises this as one of the chief concerns of the Spirit.

It is rather a shock to discover from Morton Kelsey that "Nearly one fifth of the entire Gospels is devoted to Jesus' healing and the discussions occasioned by it. Except for miracles in general, this is by far the greatest emphasis given to any one kind of experience in the narrative. It is startling to compare this emphasis on spiritual and mental healing with the scant attention given to moral healing. Very few examples of moral or ethical transformation are mentioned in the Gospels." (2)

This is not to deny the primacy of the spiritual in the New Testament; the central thing about us is always the health of our relationship to God. It is however to insist that that central relationship does not stand in isolation by itself, it is rather the key to a wholeness which, in the intention of Jesus comprehends the whole, physical, intellectual, psychological, moral and social life of man. This is because he is himself the Man, as Pilate hailed him—"Behold the Man (*ho anthropos*)" (John 19:5)—finding out of his own unique relationship to God a unique wholeness of human life. And because he is the Man, where his Spirit is renewingly active, there will not be a narrowing down of life into exercises of piety and concentration on religious concerns, but a release of creativity in every realm. This approaches Paul's emphasis in Romans 8:11, where he sees the significance of the indwelling of the Spirit for the body—the outward visible earthly expression of our human reality. "If the Spirit of him who raised Jesus from the dead dwells in you, he who raised Christ Jesus from the dead will give life to your mortal bodies also through his Spirit who dwells within you."

Whether this bodily quickening belongs to this life or the next, or, as I would maintain, to the one as the foretaste of the other, Paul is clearly looking for the emergence of the new man in all his humanity, in a resurrection which, like his own, is not a flight from the human to the 'spiritual' but the affirmation of the human, as renewed and transformed in its bodily form by the resurrecting Spirit who made, first him and now us—men.

(c) But further, it was *flesh* that the Word became; the humanity that Christ took and recreated and glorified in himself was the very humanity that in us had been ravished and ruined by sin.

At this point we do well to walk warily, since there are two vital affirmations that need to be made here, and it is so easy in making one, to seem to be denying the other. We need to affirm Christ's total sinlessness, and yet at the same time his total identification with sinners in the situation to which their sin has brought them. Hebrews holds both these together when it says, "We have not an high priest who is unable to sympathise with our weaknesses, but one who in every respect has been tempted as we are, yet without sinning" (Heb. 4:15). Let us look at each emphasis in turn:

(i) He is without sin. Jesus, in order to be who he is, remains for ever completely uncompromised in thought or deed with world, flesh and devil, in perfect obedience and undivided fellowship with his Father. We have a high priest who is "holy, blameless, unstained, separated from sinners" (Heb. 7:26). Otherwise he becomes one of us in our rebellion and sin, and so is unable to save us from them. He is entirely without sin.

(ii) But in order that his work may be relevant to our need, he enters completely into the situation of sinners, and is in every respect exposed to every external and internal pressure that comes against them. The outcome is entirely different; he stands, we fall; but the battlefield is the same.

The New Testament piles paradox upon paradox to emphasise Christ's saving entry into our plight and misery as sinners. He was made in all things like his brethren (Heb. 2:17), he became a curse for us (Gal. 3:13), he was made sin for us (II Cor. 5:21), he was sent in the likeness of sinful flesh

(Rom. 8:3). And this saving solidarity with sinners was worked out not only forensically in his death on Calvary, but realistically in his whole life in our manhood of which Calvary was the climax, in which he engaged with a human nature, over which in us sin had ruled, but in him could rule no more.

As Karl Barth puts it,

> There must be no weakening or obscuring of the saving truth that the nature which God assumed in Christ is identical with our nature, as we see it in the light of the Fall. If it was otherwise, how could Christ be really like us? What concern could we have with him? We stand before God characterised by the Fall. God's Son not only assumed our nature, but he entered the concrete form of our nature, under which we stand before God as men damned and lost. (3)

Barth is typical of much of the best modern theology of many different schools (4) in thus championing a position which Edward Irving espoused with great eloquence and at great cost almost a hundred and fifty years ago, "Our Lord took the same nature, body and soul, as other men, and under the same disadvantages of every sort, that his flesh was mortal and corruptible and passive to all temptations; that his soul was joined to his body according to the same laws, and under the same conditions, as ours is, and liable to be tempted by the objects of a fallen world, acting upon it and approaching it, through his flesh, just as ours is—in one word that his human will had lying against it and upon it, exactly the same oppressions of devil, world and flesh, which lay against and upon Adam's will, after he had fallen, and which lie upon every man's will unto this day." (5)

It can only fill us with thanksgiving and hope to realise that the Son of God took to himself this intractable flesh of ours, and in taking it regenerated it and sanctified it by the Holy Spirit, so that what in us had been the very home of sin became in him the very expression of his Father's likeness and glory. Starting with the human stuff with which we start, and confronting victoriously every temptation we have to confront, by the Holy Spirit he remade our humanity in himself and brought it home from the far country of its fallenness to God. Because this is so, we have solid foundation to believe that when our human life in all its lostness is joined to him and opened to the same Spirit, he can remake us in the same glorious likeness.

(d) But we have to look also at the possibilities that Christ opened to our humanity. We have seen that he started where we start, but he opened to us, by what he did with our manhood, new possibilities, that without him remained closed to us.

The way in which Christologies deal with Christ's miracles and mighty works is a good indication of the sort of concept of his humanity with which they are working. There are those who want to understand the possibilities that were open to him in the light of the possibilities that are open to us, as we are, and there are those who want to measure our possibilities by those that we see revealed and actualised in him. Reductionist liberalism tended to dismiss the miracles as later supernatural accretions, or to reinterpret them as ordinary human possibilities that belong to our humanity as such, and it did this basically to establish its assumption that Christ, not only at the beginning, but at the end also, was no different from us.

But the humanity that he shares with us is not to be defined in terms of what we have done with it, but in terms of what he has done with it. He is the prototype for us, not we for him.

By joining our humanity with himself in the one person of the Son of God, and by operating in it in all the freedom of the Holy Spirit, he has taken what was in the power of the world, the flesh and the devil, and so regenerated and sanctified it, that it becomes the place where the Spirit's fruits and gifts and his Father's glories are revealed. When we see the new man living in this love and acting with this authority, we see the picture and the promise of what we can be in him.

In Christ the whole fullness of the Godhead dwells bodily. This means that everything that has its origin in his divinity comes to expression in his humanity. Just as he takes our sinful flesh to himself, so he gives his divine fullness to us. The divine righteousness finds its expression in human *teleiosis*, completeness, the divine power finds its expression in human *charisma*, and within his own life every divine attribute has its human analogy, likeness and reflection in his manhood.

There has been a tendency in Protestant circles, not without its origin in Calvin, to distribute the attributes of Christ between his divinity and humanity, so that his power to work signs and miracles is seen as the power of his unique divinity. The consequence is obvious; if his miracles had nothing to do with his humanity, if divine power was not communicated to his human nature as charismatic gift, then obviously that power has nothing to do with our humanity either. It belongs to what separates him from us, rather than to that which he shares with us. With this kind of Christology all kinds of dispensationalising of the gifts of the Holy Spirit are very much at home.

But this is certainly not the way that the gospel presents the matter. Christ's explicit statement in John 14:12 is quite decisively to the effect that he who is joined to him by faith shall do the works that he did, that everything that was possible to him is possible to his people; that therefore his power does not rest solely and exclusively in his divinity, but is conferred upon his humanity. He always acts, not only as God Incarnate, but throughout as a man anointed and full of the Holy Spirit, and what by the Spirit he does in his own human nature is the basis and promise of what he will do in ours. Just as to be joined to the divine holiness means for his humanity that it becomes full of peace and love and joy, so to be joined in one person with the divine power means that he becomes a man mighty in deed and word to whom God communicates his gifts.

Thus if we wish to measure the possibilities of our humanity, whether in the realm of its sanctification or its empowering, we are not to look at ourselves and scale Christ down to us, or worship the goodness and greatness of a divinity that is in principle inaccessible to us, but we are to look at him, to behold the Man that he is, and therefore the men that we shall be in him.

(e) There is in the New Testament a clear strain of teaching that what the man Jesus was and did was the result of the operation of the Holy Spirit within and through him. It is true that the Gospels have perplexingly little to say about the Spirit, perhaps for the same reason that they have little to say about Messiahship. Perhaps Jesus guarded himself by silence from the misconceptions that could have arisen from any self-proclamation of himself as anointed Messiah, and in saying little about the Spirit, the Synoptists are only being faithful to the historical situation they are describing.

It is therefore all the more significant that the Evangelists preface and introduce the ministry of Jesus with a narrative that makes it clear that he goes out to do what lies before him as a man on whom the Spirit abides in all his fullness. Luke in particular sees the Spirit as the origin of his newborn humanity, who anoints him for his messianic ministry, who keeps him from the assaults of the enemy upon him, and is the power behind the programme of deliverance which he announces in the synagogue at Nazareth.

It is the Holy Spirit who takes the humanity which is identical with our humanity and so regenerates it and sanctifies it that it can be the human expression of the life of God and the first-fruits of a new humanity. It is when we think of the humanity of Jesus in terms of the operation of the Holy Spirit, that we can see its possibilities for us who, from the same fleshly starting point, and by the same power, can be made wholly new men in Christ.

2   But we must not stop there. To say that Jesus is a man filled with the Spirit and the prototype of all such, is to say something vitally important, but it is not to say all that needs to be said. We remember Leenhardt's statement with which we started, that

Jesus is not only the Receiver but also the Dispenser of the Spirit.

Christologies which have ignored that and concentrated exclusively upon Christ the Spirit-filled man, have never, either in ancient or modern times, been able to establish his uniqueness in the way the New Testament requires, or to maintain anything but a quantitative distinction between him and us. They have been adoptionist Christologies, which make the divinity of Christ consist in the fact that he is a man completely and entirely possessed and filled by God's Spirit.

To take a contemporary example, the Christology sketched by Dr. James Dunn in two recent articles in the *Expository Times* seems to me to be of this type and to suffer from precisely this defect. At the crucial point he recommends that we should "pass beyond the wooden, artificial phrases of the traditional Chalcedonian formulation of the two natures of Christ, to the living, human experience of the Spirit possessing and empowering Jesus in remarkable and unique degree . . . What we call the deity of Jesus was no more and no less than the Spirit of God in him." (6)

But if the divinity of Jesus consists only in his being completely and 'uniquely' filled by the Holy Spirit, then there is no principle that we can state which will establish and preserve his uniqueness. In other words, in Dunn's view there is no reason why there should not be many Spirit-filled Sons of God, at least on the way to becoming as divine as he, as the Spirit more and more fills them. If divinity means only humanity completely filled by the Spirit, then the Lordship of Jesus is fundamentally relativised, he is reduced to *primus inter pares*, the first among equals, the one who has received in fullest measure what we are all receiving in increasing measure.

Such a view seems to me to fail to take into account the New Testament emphasis that Christ is not only our brother, who stands with us as our fellow-recipient of our Father's Spirit, but he also stands over and against us as the one who gives us the Spirit. He does not send us away from himself to God in order that we may receive the Spirit, but is calling us to his Father, he also calls us to himself as the one who will baptise us with the Spirit. "If anyone is thirsty, let him come to me and drink. He who believes in me, as the Scripture says, out of his inmost being shall flow rivers of living water. This he said of the Spirit, because the Spirit was not given, because Jesus was not yet glorified" (John 7:37-39). The gift of the Spirit is essentially dependent upon his action and his passion, his glorification in death and resurrection. If he does not go away the Paraclete cannot come, but if he goes away he will send him to us. So also Acts 2:33, "He has poured out this which you see and hear."

In the New Testament the uniqueness of Christ does not consist, as has sometimes been thought, in his keeping to himself something—e.g. the divine power to work miracles—which he does not share with us. It consists precisely in the fact that he shares everything that he has with us, but in the sharing he confronts us not only as our human brother who receives with us, but as God, who stands with his Father on the other side of the relationship and, out of the divine life that he shares with the Father, imparts the Spirit to us.

The Christology of Chalcedon is certainly not explicit in the passages we have quoted, but the experience that generated that Christology certainly is. Those who today are moving in the power of the Spirit may disagree about the adequacy of the 'wooden' and 'artificial' Chalcedonian categories to express intellectually what they have learnt of Christ, but they have certainly shared an experiential relationship with Christ, which reveals him as both the human brother who shares the gift and the divine Son who confers it, in all the freedom and majesty of his Father's love. What we have received is what only God can give us, and Jesus Christ is the essential and necessary agent of that giving. The Spirit we have received is the Spirit of Christ, and in the New Testament, that means both the Spirit that was given to Jesus of Nazareth, and the Spirit that the Son of God, who is Jesus of Nazareth, gives to us. The Pentecostal experience leads us to

affirm both Christ the true Man, whose humanity we share, and
Christ the divine Son, whose deity we adore.

Professor T. F. Torrance sums for us thus, "It behoved Jesus
Christ to be God that he might give his Spirit to men, for only God
can give God. It behoved Christ also to be Man, that he might
receive the Spirit of God in our human nature and mediate it to
his brethren through himself." (7)

We may illustrate our conclusions by an incident related by
Dr. Gordon Strachan in his *The Pentecostal Theology of Edward
Irving* (8). Mary Campbell was a theologically literate invalid in
the West of Scotland when in the late 1820s she came under the
influence of Irving's teaching about the humanity of Christ. Irving
describes what happened as follows, "She saw the truth of our
Lord's human nature, which in itself was no other than our own,
and derives the virtues of immaculate holiness and superhuman
powers from no passive quality, but from an active operation
thereon of the Son of God by the Holy Ghost . . . The Person is the
Son of God; the bounds which he hath consented to speak and act
in are the bounds of mortal manhood, the power with which,
when within these narrow bounds, he doth such mighty things . . .
is the power of the Holy Ghost; and the end of the whole mystery
of his Incarnation is to show unto mortal men what every one of
them, through faith in his name shall be able to perform . . .
[Mary Campbell] straightway argued, if Jesus as a man in my
nature thus spake and thus performed mighty works by the Holy
Ghost, which he even promiseth me, then ought I in the same
nature, by the same Spirit to do likewise the works which he did
and greater works than these." (9) Having thus argued with
herself Mary Campbell first began to speak in tongues and then
rose from her bed healed.

There could be no clearer connection between sound teaching
about Christ's person and humanity and the recovery of spiritual
gifts. She had found in Irving's charismatic Christology a *relevant*
Christ, who operated in a humanity that was the same as hers by

the power of the Spirit that he was ready to confer upon her. It is such a Christology, whose various implications we shall press on to explain in greater detail, that provides the essential basis for spiritual renewal, by anchoring it in him whose manhood is the original and chief work of the Spirit, and who in his divine freedom promises to bestow the Spirit on all who come to him.

Notes to Chapter Five

NOTES

1 Franz J. Leenhardt, *The Epistle to the Romans* (Lutterworth), p. 37

2 Morton T. Kelsey, *Healing and Christianity* (S.C.M.), p. 54

3 Karl Barth, *Church Dogmatics* (T. & T. Clark), I. 2 p. 53

4 c.f. Torrance, *Theology in Reconstruction* (S.C.M.), p. 132
Wolfhart Pannenberg, *Jesus God and Man* (S.C.M.), p. 362
Lesslie Newbigin, *Sin and Salvation* (S.C.M.), p. 60
And all the impressive array of authorities mustered by Harry Johnson, *The Humanity of the Saviour* (Epworth), 1962—a fascinating study of this whole theme.

5 Edward Irving, *The Opinions Circulating Concerning our Lord's Human Nature* (London 1830) pp. 3–4

6 James D. G. Dunn, "Rediscovering the Spirit" Part II *Expository Times*, (Nov. 1972), p. 11

7 T. F. Torrance, *Theology in Reconstruction* (S.C.M.) p. 245

8 C. Gordon Strachan, *The Pentecostal Theology of Edward Irving* (Darton, Longman & Todd), pp. 64–69

9 Edward Irving, *Facts Connected with Recent Manifestations of Spiritual Gifts* (London, 1832) p. 757

CHAPTER SIX

Birth and Baptism in the Spirit

THE KIND of Christological approach towards which we have been feeling emphasises the work of the Holy Spirit in the humanity of Jesus, and so the connection between his human experience and ours. To grasp with new clarity the relationship between Christ's humanity and the Spirit was one of the essential insights of Edward Irving's Christological work, completed almost a hundred and fifty years ago, but only now coming into its own.

Irving works entirely within the framework of Chalcedonian orthodoxy, but the 'woodenness' and 'artificiality' of which James Dunn and others have complained, is largely removed by the dynamic and relevant way in which he presents the whole inter-action of the human and the divine in Christ.

Classical Christologies have tended to set the two natures of Christ in such paradoxical relationship to each other, that the unity of his Person and the reality of his life have often seemed ambiguous and unconvincing. But Irving, when he wants to deal with the relationship between the divine Person who is the subject of the Incarnation and the human nature he assumes, speaks of the Holy Spirit. Just as the Holy Spirit is the 'Go-between' between Father and Son in the life of the Trinity, and between Head and Body in the life of the Church, so is he, between the divinity and the humanity in the one person of the Incarnate Son. Jesus is what he is and does what he does, not in some static balance of ontological forces, but in the ongoing interaction of the Son of God upon his humanity in the Holy Spirit.

Irving believed that the relevance of Christ's humanity to ours could be understood in two ways. First, because by the action of the Holy Spirit, the Son of God entered our real manhood and so lived on our scene under our conditions, "We present believers with a real life, suffering mortal flesh; a real death and a real resurrection of this flesh of ours." (1) Second, the Spirit who operated in his manhood works also i   rs. Irving held it to be "the sum and substance of sound theology; that the Lord Jesus Christ, in virtue of his Incarnation and humiliation to the death, hath received from the Father the gift of the Holy Spirit—regeneration, resurrection, and eternal life with all power in heaven and on earth: which now lie all treasured up in him, not for selfish enjoyment, but right welcome communication unto every one who hath received faith from the Father to apprehend and possess them." (2)

Irving's Christology has been given detailed exposition by Dr. Gordon Strachan. Whatever criticism and correction it may require, it offers a basically dynamic, charismatic and practical representation of the Person of Christ that can provide the modern charismatic renewal with a far sounder basis than the second blessing Pentecostalism on which it has hitherto too much relied.

On that general Christological basis, we have now to look at different aspects of the work of the Spirit, originally in Jesus and then in us. In the New Testament we can see that the Spirit performs both in Christ and in us a work of initiation—by the Spirit he is made Christ, and by the same Spirit we are made Christians. It is at this that we must now look. When we do, two blocks of New Testament material immediately come to mind—the Gospel accounts first of his birth and then of his baptism, in both of which the Holy Spirit plays a decisive part. By birth and by baptism he is instituted into his ministry.

It is interesting that all four Gospels speak of his baptism, whereas only two record his birth, and that fact is suggestive of the relationship between them, which we could formulate by saying that his birth is the hidden presupposition of his baptism, and his baptism is the explication of his birth.

If the birth that Matthew and Luke record, and which in its own way John 1:14 records again, had been followed by nothing but the quiet and uneventful life of the uncalled carpenter of Nazareth, there would have been a deep contradiction between the beginning and what followed from it. A birth like that needed a sequel to make sense of it. On the other hand, if he who in his baptism was called to and anointed for his messianic vocation, was not also the one who came from God, and not from man, and had his beginning in divine mystery rather than in human heredity, then the whole character of the story is changed in an adoptionist direction. To understand his baptism we have to presuppose his birth.

I can only partly agree with Dr. James Dunn when he says that "Jesus' birth belongs entirely to the old covenant, the epoch of Israel. Luke makes this very plain: the first two chapters are entirely Old Testament in character and even in thought and phraseology," (3) and "Jesus' anointing with the Spirit . . . is in fact the event which begins the new covenant for Jesus, it initiates the messianic age and initiates Jesus into the messianic age." (4)

It is certainly true that the birth of Jesus takes place in the context of Old Testament Israel, but to say that it belongs entirely to the old covenant is to miss its essential nature. By it the new has been mysteriously and secretly inserted into the old, so that few knew of it, and they only by specific revelation, but it is still true that "Unto you is born this day in the city of David a Saviour, who is Christ the Lord" (Luke 2:11). From the moment when the maiden bears her son, his name is to be called Emmanuel, which means that in a new way and in a new covenant God is with us (Matthew 1:23). For thirty years the new lies in wait amidst the old for the hour of his appearing but the basis for all that is to follow has been laid in the miracle of Christmas, in the act of the Holy Spirit in the Virgin Mary that has brought forth the new man.

We cannot here begin to enter into all questions that arise in connection with the birth of Jesus, both in terms of biblical exegesis and of the history of doctrine. But that need not stop us from exploring its theological and Christological significance, and from seeing that what is recorded in this almost incredible start to the gospel story is in deep unity with all that follows after.

The virgin birth of Jesus proclaims that something has been done in our humanity which it could not do for itself, something has been given to it which it could not give to itself. Man, as he is, is to the roots of his being in deep rebellion against God, dead in sins and trespasses, incapable of right relationship and response to God. As Barth puts it, "This human nature, the only one we know and the only one there actually is, has of itself no capacity for being adopted by God's Word into unity with Himself, i.e. into personal unity with God. Upon this human nature a mystery must be wrought in order that this may be made possible. And this mystery must consist in its receiving the capacity for God which it does not possess." (5)

Mary and Joseph cannot of themselves bring forth the new humanity which can be the temple of God's glory. Mary cannot be the mother of the Son of God in virtue of anything in herself, but only in virtue of the favour shown her and the power that comes upon her and overshadows her, and forms in her what will be called the Son of God (Luke 1:35). She brings nothing of her own; the child, and the willingness to receive the child are the work in her of the Word who through the Spirit is to become flesh in her —flesh, that is still our flesh with the inheritance of our flesh, but now given grace to be united in one life with God. All this is the work of the Holy Spirit, he is "conceived by the Holy Ghost".

As Barth again puts it, "Through the Holy Spirit and only through the Holy Spirit can man be there for God, be free for God's work on him, believe, be a recipient of this revelation, the object of the divine reconciliation ... The very possibility of human nature's being adopted into unity with the Son of God is the Holy Ghost ... Through the Spirit it becomes really possible for the creature, for man, to be there and to be free for God." (6)

Thus at the basis of the Word's becoming flesh is a regenerating act of the Holy Spirit upon that flesh, giving it a possibility that is not its own and can come to it only by the action of undeserved divine favour—union with God.

But the actual content of what it means to be God's Son in man's flesh, the actual calling which sets in action his whole ministry and mission, the experiential entry into the vocation that awaits him, and therefore the explication of the miracle of Christmas belongs to Christ's baptism in Jordan. It is there—and here we agree with Dunn—that Jesus is personally inaugurated and publicly instituted into his messianic office, and the new covenant emerges from its thirty year hiding in the midst of the old in what Dunn rightly calls one of the pivotal events of the whole gospel story.

For here the glory of God is provisionally revealed in all its dimensions. The Father acknowledges the Son and bestows the Spirit. Here what was already event in his birth becomes conscious experience in his baptism; he who was born of the Spirit comes to know the energising and enabling work of the Spirit within him. Now, in continuity with what has gone before, and yet with new conscious participation he can say "The Spirit of the Lord is upon me" (Luke 4:18).

Here in his initiation, the whole course of his ministry is prefigured in such a way that from this point it proceeds on its distinctive way through his life, death, and rising to its eschatological culmination.

(a) In his baptism there is prefiguration of the cross. Here he identifies himself with the repentant sinners who have responded to John's preaching, and goes down with them into a baptism of repentance insisting, in spite of John's protests, that he is under obligation "To fulfill all righteousness" (Matthew 3:15). He is in a real sense baptised in Jordan into his identification with sinners, and so into his death, so that he can later speak of his death as a baptism (Mark 10:38).

(b) In his baptism there is a prefiguration of the resurrection. As he accompanies the old man down into his death, so he brings up the new man to newness of life (Romans 6:4) and as he emerges from the water, so he is confirmed in the status that belongs to him, "Thou art my beloved Son; with thee I am well pleased" (Luke 3:22) quoting Psalm 2:7. This connects with the resurrection by way of Romans 1:4, "designated Son of God in power according to the Spirit of holiness by his resurrection from the dead"—a verse that also attests the connection between the Spirit and the resurrection; and we have only to continue the quotation from Psalm 2 to see how it points to his ascended rule and glory, "Ask of me and I will make the nations your heritage, and the ends of the earth your possession" (Psa. 2:7–8).

(c) In his baptism there is prefiguration of Pentecost, because here he receives the Spirit for the work that lies ahead of him. Not that he was without the Spirit until now; both his birth and his boyhood were full of the Spirit, but now the Spirit, in the full release of the dawning Messianic age, moves into that position in his humanity where he will be able fully to manifest the presence and power of God.

There is no basis whatever in the story for making the descent of the Spirit upon Jesus merely symbolic or revelatory in import. The text speaks clearly of a real impartation of the Spirit, a new liberating of the Spirit for a whole new phase not only of Jesus's human life but of God's eternal purpose. Here Jesus is inaugurated as God's Messiah anointed with God's Spirit, and this is the basic presupposition of his whole ministry. It is not often stated explicitly in the accounts of that ministry that his authority (*exousia*) and power (*dunamis*) have the Spirit as their source. But the baptism story, the testimony of Jesus at Nazareth (Luke 4:18) and Peter's statement to Cornelius (Acts 10:38) make it quite clear that what happened as he came up out of Jordan is the key to all that was to follow.

Also, one cannot fail to see in the picture of the Christ anointed with the Spirit the further promise of the Christians, anointed with the same Spirit and power on the day of Pentecost. John's words make that promise explicit. "He who is now being baptised will baptise you with the Holy Spirit"—and it is in conscious fulfilment of that prophecy of John that Jesus makes his own promise of Pentecost (Acts 1:5).

So, in his baptism that which is basic to his birth is unfolded, and he is initiated into a proleptic experience of all that lies ahead of him. In the power and love of the Spirit he will go to his death and resurrection and inaugurate the age of the Spirit. For all this was Jesus born, and into the anticipation of all this he was baptised.

As the Spirit operates originally in the Head, so does he reflect what has been done in the Head in the members; as he has brought the Christ to birth and baptism, so does he bring the Christian to a birth like his and a baptism like his.

F. D. Bruner rejects the validity of our analogy between the virgin birth of Christ and the regeneration of Christians, and apparently imagines that to draw it is some Pentecostal peculiarity, whereas this has been regularly done in Reformed circles and elsewhere as well. (7) Bruner writes, "One may wonder if there is not a certain lack of sensitivity in Pentecostals paralleling their own conversion with Jesus' virgin birth," and then more strongly, "We must interpret the Pentecostals' comparison of their regeneration with Jesus' virgin birth . . . as unfounded, and then as unfortunate and Christologically inappropriate." (8)

One can only say that, far from being unfortunate, the parallel is very much to the point. Both the birth of Christ and the rebirth of Christians are works of the Holy Spirit in giving a new capacity for relationship and response to God to our fallen humanity. And, far from being unfounded, the parallel is almost explicitly and quite unmistakably drawn out in John 1:12 where believers are described as "children of God; who were born not of blood, nor of the will of the flesh, nor of the will of a man (*andros* = male) but of God." One could also quote John 3, where the same imagery is used in a baptismal context, "Unless a man is born again of water and the Spirit, he cannot enter into the kingdom of God."

The making of a Christian, like the making of the Christ, is a creative miraculous act of the Holy Spirit, giving our nature a capacity for God that in its fallenness it does not have, and cannot give itself. So James 1:18, "Of his own will he brought us forth by the word of truth," and 1 Peter 1:23, "You have been born anew, not of perishable seed but of imperishable, through the living and abiding word of God"—in both of which the action of the living Word is equivalent to the action of the Holy Spirit in the Johannine texts.

Regeneration is mentioned in the New Testament much less than faith or repentance. Perhaps the emphasis falls less on regeneration than on confession of faith, for the very same reason that the birth of Jesus is less emphasised than his baptism; namely that the two former are the very necessary but also the hidden presuppositions of the two latter.

Like the birth of Jesus, the regeneration of the Christian is less a matter of conscious spiritual experience, than the real, but hidden and mysterious event which is the presupposition and the basis of all the conscious experiences that flow from it. We become Christians not by feeling that a re-creative act has been performed at the depth of our being, but when we believe in Christ and confess him and turn to him in repentance, and it is by these conscious acts that we enter into actual experience of the new life that has been made ours.

But the doctrine of new birth by the Spirit through the word reminds us, that our response to the gospel through faith, confession and repentance, is not something that is at the disposal of our own choice; these are not natural human possibilities open to fallen sinners, but are possibilities that have to be given to us by the re-creating activity of the Holy Spirit upon us. Just as Jesus can only be acknowledged as God's Son at his baptism because his humanity was regenerated by the Holy Spirit at his birth, so we can only believe and repent on the presupposition that there has been deep in our being a mysterious regenerating act of the Holy Spirit, making us sons.

This emphasis on regeneration as the basis of conversion is important because it acknowledges an act of grace and the work of the Holy Spirit as the basis of the Christian life. This has so often been obscured in modern American-type evangelism, which has laid all the stress on human decision, and seen the new birth as something God gives in response to a prior act of human faith. When all the stress is laid on free human decision in this way, it is in the last resort we who choose to make ourselves Christians, and who take ourselves out of the realm of sin into the realm of the Spirit. Such a view contrasts vividly with the emphasis of the New Testament, "You he made alive when you were dead in trespasses and sins . . . But God who is rich in mercy, out of the great love with which he loved us, even when we were dead through our trespasses, made us alive together with Christ . . . For by grace you have been saved through faith, and this is not your own doing it is the gift of God." (Eph. 2:1, 4, 5, 8). Here the whole emphasis is on the gracious action of God in bringing dead men to life, in working in us a miracle of resurrection of which we were by definition incapable, so that being made alive, we could then come to Christ.

It is not surprising that modern evangelism of this type, for all its impressive statistics of decisions, has had such difficulty in holding those it claims to have won, when it puts so much weight on such a fragile basis as human decision for Christ. And, more central to our own concern, it is not surprising that when the Christian life is understood as having its origin in a human choice of faith, it should also be seen to continue through human efforts after faithfulness, obedience, sanctification, where no doubt the Spirit appears as subsidiary helper at each stage, but where the initiative is seen to rest upon us, so that we are urged to a series of decisive steps towards our own consecration, and promised his help only when we have taken them. The decisive human initiative backed up by the assisting divine grace, has been the pattern of so much personal Christianity and of church life, and so much preaching has been endless demand for people to produce a faith, love and power that they know was not in them to produce, and that has therefore left them unheeding or disconsolate.

Such Arminian attitudes seem to me to be radically out of sympathy with the charismatic emphasis. One side is saying, "You must, and then God will help you," whereas the other is saying a much more radical, "You can't, but God can." If the Christian life is initiated by an act of human decision, it follows that it must be sustained by further acts of human decision, and the fullness of the Holy Spirit is at best the final blessing at the end of a long long road. It was this sort of emphasis that F. D. Bruner was attacking when he rightly saw the Pentecostal teaching about 'conditions for receiving' as being inconsistent with the doctrine of grace. What he failed to see was that this attitude is caused by the Arminian background of much Pentecostal theology, rather than in anything inherent in the Pentecostal experience as such.

Where the beginning of the Christian life is seen to be the regenerating work of the Holy Spirit, it is consistent to see the whole Christian life as being radically dependent upon the Spirit, his gift, provision and power. If it is by the creative act of God, and not our own, that we become Christians, we shall naturally look to the continued action of God to maintain us and make us effective Christians.

None of this is to minimise in any way the vital importance of faith, repentance, confession of Christ. These are the conscious acts and outward manifestations of the hidden work of regeneration. The born-again man says with the first breath he draws, "Abba, Father," "Jesus is Lord." If he did not, his regeneration would mean precisely nothing. But the point is that his faith, his repentance and his confession are not acts of the natural man, any more than the acts of Jesus Christ in his baptism are the acts of the natural man. They point back to the miracle of God in that life, by the Word and through the Spirit; they are the experiential fruits of the regenerating act of the Spirit. To repent, to confess, to close with Christ, we must be born again.

To insist on all this is not to solve all the problems of human freedom and divine predestination that inevitably arise at this point. It is simply to point out, that whatever the problems and the answers to them may be, if we are to speak with the New Testament about the beginning of the Christian life, we dare not speak exclusively of human decision, or let the emphasis fall there. Just as it was God's initiative and act that made Christ, so it is God's initiative and act that bring us into regenerate relationship to Christ. "You did not choose me, but I chose you and appointed you that you should go and bear fruit and that your fruit should abide" (John 15:16).

We have distinguished two factors in Christ's initiation into his Messiahship, the event of his birth in its comparative hiddenness, and the experience of his baptism as the unfolding of what is involved in his birth. We are now seeing that the same two factors are involved in our initiation into Christ. They are clearly indicated in their distinction and connection in John 3:5, "Unless a man is born again of water and the Spirit, he cannot enter the kingdom of God."

At the beginning there is the mystery of rebirth which is the result of the free and mysterious act of the Pneuma, the Spirit/Wind who blows where he wills (John 3:8) and then as a result of that there is the experienced conscious act of "entering the kingdom". There could be no better description of the baptism of Jesus; in it the Messiah King, who has been born of the Spirit, enters into his kingdom, and comes to grips with the nature of that kingdom as it is prefigured in his baptism. As suffering Servant he closes with his cross, as favoured Son he looks to his exaltation and victory, receives the Holy Spirit in power to exercise his ministry and bestows the same Spirit upon his people.

Thus in conformity with his Lord, the Christian who is born again of the Spirit, comes, by the activity of the Spirit, to the point of faith, repentance and confession, where he experiences his entry into the kingdom. At this point what the Spirit has already done within him becomes explicit and outward.

In the New Testament the context of that initiation, for the Christian as well as for Christ, is baptism; it is in this form that the Christian confesses the grace of God that has taken hold of him in Christ, turns to Christ in repentance, and is joined to the Body over whom Christ rules as Head.

New Testament baptism marks the initiation of believers into conscious participation in Christ and his kingdom through a faith that enables them to experience all that the gospel promises. The initiatory event is both as effective and as incomplete and proleptic as was Christ's in Jordan. He has far to travel still in his experience of cross, resurrection and Spirit, but he has from this point on decisively opened himself to them, and they have begun to shape his life. By the baptismal confession of Christ which is the result of the regenerating act of the Spirit, he has been constituted and acknowledged as a Christian. He has confessed with his lips that Jesus is Lord and believed in his heart that God raised him from the dead—and so he is saved (Romans 10:9).

So the regenerate, confessing Christian begins, from his initiation into Christ, to experience the same dimensions of the kingdom as Jesus experienced in his. He begins to enter into both the grace and the claim of the cross; he is baptised into the death of Christ, which both offers him forgiveness and calls him to take up his own cross and follow Christ. He is baptised into newness of life, into Christ's resurrection, and shares with Christ his status as God's son; he is baptised into the outpoured Holy Spirit and commissioned and empowered for Christ's witness and service. Jesus the crucified Saviour, the risen Lord, the anointed Christ, imparts his Spirit and begins by that Spirit to conform the Christian to his likeness. "Do you not know that all of us who have been baptised into Christ Jesus were baptised into his death? We were buried therefore with him by baptism into death, so that as Christ was raised from the dead by the glory of the Father, we too might walk in newness of life" (Rom. 6:4). And to make explicit the relationship of this to the Spirit we have only to remind ourselves again of Acts 2:38, "Be baptised ... and you shall receive the gift of the Holy Spirit"—where the context is Pentecostal and the only possible interpretation of what receiving the gift of the Spirit involves is the experience of the apostles that day.

Thus we can say that in the New Testament initiation into Christ includes at least three distinguishable elements:

1 Its basis—the regenerating act of the Spirit bringing us to new birth in analogy to Christ's birth.

2 A resultant entry by confession, repentance and faith into experiential participation in Christ, crucified and risen and in the Holy Spirit.

3 The expression and proclamation of this in the rite of being baptised in water.

The above is to be understood as theological analysis rather than as a description of a temporal sequence. I am in full agreement with Dr. James Dunn when he says that there is no systematic factor in the thirty years gap between Jesus's birth and baptism that could be turned into the basis for a second blessing theology. The different sequences in Acts where the same elements appear in different temporal combinations warn us to leave the Spirit his freedom at this point.

Nor do I wish here to take any stand on the relationship of the sacramental aspect—water-baptism—to the other two, whether it must necessarily precede (paedo-baptism) or follow (believers' baptism) our experiential participation in Christ, and how it is related to our regeneration. The baptism that Peter offered on the day of Pentecost was a baptism that was simultaneous with regeneration and experience of Christ and the Spirit. In Church history baptism and conversion have tended to be separated from one another, and in more catholic traditions baptism into Christ has tended again to be separated from full reception of the Spirit at confirmation, so that the wholeness of Christian initiation has been broken up into temporally separate parts—in a way not all that different from Pentecostalist second blessing teaching.

It may be that the renewal of the Church will result in God's joining together again what man has put asunder, that the miracle of rebirth in which God acts by the Spirit, and the experiential entry by faith and repentance into the fullness of Christ that result from the rebirth, and the sacramental act which proclaims and affirms our union with Christ, will again be seen in their essential oneness as the way by which we enter into our inheritance and see the kingdom of God.

Notes to Chapter Six

NOTES

1 Edward Irving, *Christ's Holiness in Flesh* (London, 1831) Preface, p. v

2 Edward Irving, *The Sealing Virtue of Baptism* Collected Works, Vol. II, p. 279

3 James D. G. Dunn, *Baptism in the Holy Spirit* (S.C.M.), p. 31

4 Ibid. pp. 24–25

5 Karl Barth, *Church Dogmatics* (T. and T. Clark), I. 2. pp. 188–9

6 Ibid. pp. 198–9

7 e.g. Karl Barth, *The Faith of the Church* (Fontana), pp. 107–8 William Temple, *Readings in St. John's Gospel* (Macmillan), p. 13. Hoskyns and Davey, *The Fourth Gospel* (Faber & Faber), pp. 164–5

8 F. D. Bruner, *A Theology of the Holy Spirit* (Hodder & Stoughton), p. 122

CHAPTER SEVEN

Attack and Authority

IF WE take up the three elements of the calling into which Jesus was baptised—cross, resurrection and Spirit—in reverse order, we shall in fact be following the gospel material, especially in Luke's presentation. As Luke follows Jesus from his baptismal initiation into the events of his ministry, he speaks first of the Holy Spirit.

In particular, he prefaces his account of Jesus's temptation with a quite explicit reference to the work of the Spirit, "And Jesus, full of the Holy Spirit, returned from Jordan, and was led by the Spirit for forty days in the wilderness, tempted by the devil." (Luke 4:1-2) The same verse and the narrative that follows make it quite clear that in speaking explicitly of the Spirit, we are still dealing implicitly with both the cross and the resurrection. The contradiction between 'led by the Spirit' and 'tempted by the devil' is the beginning of the contradiction which will ultimately construct Calvary; and the superiority of Spirit to devil, which the conclusion of the story demonstrates, is the ultimate basis of Christ's Easter victory. Here in his trial, he makes choices that will ultimately bring him to the cross and to his rising.

The Epistle to the Hebrews says that Jesus was "in every respect tempted as we are" (Heb. 4:15), but these particular temptations are not the common lot of all men, as anyone who has tried to make them real to an adolescent Bible class well knows. They are temptations special to Christ's Messianic mission, and make sense only in relation to the calling and gift of the Spirit he has received.

These are, in other words, the peculiar temptations of the Spirit-filled Christ. Their context is not merely moral, but the eschatological clash of the power of the enemy against the purpose of God, so that the newly called and empowered Jesus can be diverted from his Father's will and the world's salvation. One of the great ministries of the Spirit is our sanctification, not in the general moral sense of making us good—but in the eschatological and messianic sense of separating us from all that disqualifies us from God's purpose with us, and, positively, of consecrating us and making us available for God's service. Here the struggle between Spirit and flesh is represented in its prototypal and ultimate form as the struggle between God's incarnate Son and Satan.

To understand the meaning of his temptation for his mission and ours we must take the following points into account:

1 The *reality* of the temptation. This was a real attack, and not play-acting. The enemy who came upon the first Adam and conquered, comes again against the last Adam and, as Barth points out (1), exercises a remarkable power and initiative over him, proposing alternative after alternative to him, taking him to both the temple and the mountain and determining the whole trend of the dialogue between them. This story speaks not of the immunity of Jesus, but of his vulnerability, his real entry into a real fight in which tremendous issues were at stake.

Jesus was vulnerable because he came to the fight, not as the disincarnate Son of God who cannot be tempted, but, as Paul puts it in Romans 8:3, "in the likeness of sinful flesh" (*en hoiomati sarkos hamartias*). "In that expression," says Nygren, "there is no trace of docetism. Christ's carnal nature was no unreality, but simple tangible fact. He shared all our conditions. He was under the same powers of destruction. Out of 'the flesh' arose for him the same temptations as for us." (2) His flesh, though regenerated into unity with his Person, was, like our regenerate flesh, still open to the suggestions of its hereditary enemy, and, apart from his grace, still liable to listen and to fall. This is only to say, that his victory was won in a situation that is in every respect identical with ours. He was "*in every respect* tempted as we are".

The ordinary man's reaction to the story of Jesus's victory over his temptations is, "It was different for him, because he was God's Son," and if Christ's humanity had a built-in immunity to sin then indeed it was totally different for him. The devil's attacks were only useless popguns vainly trying to prevent the iron horses of the divine purpose from going on their irresistible way. But of course, it was no different for him; he was in our situation, both internally and externally, and felt every pressure that we can feel— and yet conquered. This leads to the second point which has to do with:

2   The *relevance* of his victory. If it was a victory won in a situation different from ours with resources unavailable to us, then it was, as far as we are concerned, an irrelevant victory. Christ was fighting, not our battle as our representative, but some completely different battle of his own.

But he was in our situation and in it "yet without sin". He neither did nor could sin, because he brought to bear on our shared situation all the energy and grace of the Holy Spirit to work overcomingly and sanctifyingly in our flesh. All the power the enemy can bring against us was marshalled against him, but it was all resisted and negatived, because, though in the flesh and with complete 'likeness' to the flesh, he did not walk in the flesh nor do what the flesh does. "The law of the Spirit of life in Christ Jesus has set me free from the law of sin and death" (Rom. 8:2). That law worked like that in the life of Paul because it operated first like that in the temptations of Jesus. His victory over sin—and this was a point that in his day Edward Irving never tired of making—was not in virtue of some miracle of immunity, which is certainly not repeated in us, but in virtue of the operation of the Son of God upon the flesh he had assumed in the sanctifying power of the Holy Spirit.

"This is the substance of our argument—that his human nature was holy in the only way in which holiness under the Fall exists or can exist—through inworking or energising of the Holy Ghost." (3)

So Jesus's identification with us in his temptation is complete. He takes our flesh in all its reality and gives us his Spirit in all his sanctifying energy, and with the same sanctity with which he made holy his own nature, he begins to sanctify ours—and does it, be it noted, often in the same way in which he won his own victory, through the power of the word ("It is written . . ." Luke 4:4, 8, 12).

We are not to be surprised if being initiated with Christ into the full flood of the Spirit soon leads us into the wilderness where we have to face our own share of the conflict of the Spirit against the flesh. The charismatic honeymoon soon passes, and the warfare in the wilderness begins, but this is not a sign that something has gone wrong, but rather a sign that the great battle with the flesh in which Christ engaged immediately after his experience in Jordan is breaking out in us also.

So also our victory is in him, and not in ourselves; it is a reflection of his victory worked in us by his Spirit. "Because he himself has suffered and been tempted, he is able to help those who are tempted" (Heb. 2:18).

3 We should also note the *form* of his temptation—which relates directly to the baptism that precedes it. There Jesus had been acknowledged Son of God and, as such, anointed with the Holy Spirit. The whole thrust of his temptation, above and beyond its specific content, is to separate his employment of the Spirit's power from his status and vocation of Sonship. To use the power of the Spirit in a sanctified way is to use it as a Son, and the attack of the tempter is calculated to cast doubt in different ways upon his vocation as Son. "*If* you are the Son of God . . ." (Luke 4:3, 9). Unbelief in God's vocation leads to misuse of God's gifts. The gift of the Holy Spirit, far from being the result of an already achieved sanctification, itself raises the issue of sanctification in its most acute form—what are we going to do with the power that

God has given us? Shall we use our Father's gifts as our Father's children?

(a) Christ's first temptation is to *presume* on his Sonship—to use the spiritual power which he has received for his own self-satisfaction, to make the stones bread in order that his own hunger may be met. His response, from the word, is that man does not live in the satisfying of his own needs, but in obedience to the will and purpose of God.

Where the power of the Spirit is valued chiefly in terms of the self-fulfilment it can provide, where the gospel offer of wholeness is corrupted into a demand for instant solutions to everything that is a problem or a nuisance, where people are constantly athirst for new religious experiences and gifts to slake their endless spiritual curiosity—there Corinthian charismatic carnality reappears; the genuine gifts of God are taken into bondage by the self-assertion of man, and the Spirit-filled man falls to the first temptation from which only a fresh grasp of Christ and his messianic mission can rescue him.

(b) Christ's second temptation (in Luke's order) is to *abandon* his Sonship. Jesus's Sonship is just not mentioned, when the devil takes him up into the high mountain and offers him the kingdoms of the earth and their glory. This is temptation to become obsessed by power, in and for itself, and not to be too careful about the source from which it comes, the way in which it is exercised, or the purpose which it serves. It is the temptation to be undiscriminating between the devil's supernatural and God's, to be avid for remarkable words and wonderful healings without asking in whose name they are spoken and in whose power they are done. It is a refusal to test the spirits and see which are of God (1 John 4:1), it is to become unscrupulous about the way you use power to manipulate people for your own purposes, so that your ministry and your greatness will be recognised.

Its correction is to see, as the Spirit showed Jesus from the word, that the exercise of spiritual power needs to be constantly disciplined by a quite puritanical exclusiveness of concern for God's will and purpose and glory, "You shall worship the Lord your God and him only shall you serve" (Luke 4:8).

(c) Christ's third temptation is to *prove* his Sonship—to use charismatic power to establish spiritual status. The tempter tries to bring Jesus to the point at which he is so uncertain of his Father's acknowledgment of him as his Son in his baptism, that he will try to prove it to himself in a sensational way by throwing himself from the pinnacle of the temple.

It is still to this temptation that people fall, when they try to use charismatic power to establish spiritual superiority, when the man with the pentecostal experience and who, perhaps, speaks in tongues, becomes condemnatory of his fellow Christians who do neither and gives himself out, implicitly or explicitly as a first-class Christian, in a bracket above them. In so doing he betrays his obsession with status, and so his uncertainty about his own, as does equally the fierce resentment of the man without the experience or the gifts, who feels that his own status is being threatened, and is not sure enough about it to be able to meet the threat.

But in fact our sonship and our status do not rest upon, and so have no need to be proved by our possession or exercise of spiritual gifts. We are sons because God has declared us so in his word, and especially in his Word made broken flesh in the cross and resurrected flesh at Easter. The divisiveness that spiritual gifts can cause in churches is due to the pride and prejudice generated by this false connection between status and gifts, which itself rests on unbelief in God's word.

The Holy Spirit witnesses with our spirits that we are children of God (Rom. 8:16) and we are to believe that witness and not go about putting it to the test. Those who have been regenerated by the Spirit, and confessed Christ are all now the children of God, and if some have explored the riches of our inheritance more than others, that suggests no superiority, because it is an inheritance that is ours only by grace and gift, and that is freely available to all our Father's children.

In these three ways Christ was tempted from his vocation. A Christ who is concerned to satisfy his hunger, to assert his power, to prove his status, will never be about his Father's business, and will certainly never be ready for his sacrifice and for the cross where he must thirst unsatisfied, where all his power becomes weakness, where his status seems finally to be lost, and where again the tempter's voice is heard, "If you are the king of the Jews, save yourself" (Luke 23:37).

A Church, however charismatic, that wants to satisfy its own needs with God's provision, glory in its own rediscovered power and trumpet its own superiority, will by those very facts be disqualified from participating in Christ's messianic mission. Its spiritual baptism and gifts will avail it nothing, because, at the instigation of the enemy, they will have been prostituted to wrong purposes and so have become spiritually of no effect.

But Christ overcame; and the Spirit who led him through his temptation is also free in the Church, and seeks to sanctify the Church, and make Christ's wilderness victory available to us, so that we shall not lapse into charismatic carnality, but learn to live in all responsibility, loyalty and confidence of our sonship and so be qualified for Christ's service.

F. D. Bruner concludes his comments on the Temptation with the extraordinary statement that in it Jesus refused "these impressive evidences (i.e. miracles and powerful enduements) and remained instead in the quiet assurance of sonship which is baptism". (4) If this is taken to mean (a) that Jesus' baptism consisted solely in the conveying to him of the 'quiet assurance of sonship' and (b) that he repudiated the use of outward manifestations of the Spirit's power, both are completely refuted by the actual account of the baptism, which makes it clear that its essential nature was an anointing with the Holy Spirit and power, and by the sequel to the temptations, which tells not only that

Jesus "returned in the power of the Spirit into Galilee" (Luke 4:14) but of his sermon at Nazareth and the announcing in it of a programme, which consisted precisely in the performance of mighty works of power in the manifested energy of the Holy Spirit. "The Spirit of the Lord is upon me, because he has anointed me to preach good news to the poor. He has sent me to proclaim release to the captives and recovering of sight to the blind, to set at liberty those who are oppressed, to proclaim the acceptable year of the Lord . . . And he began to say to them 'Today this scripture has been fulfilled in your hearing'." (Luke 4:18, 19, 21).

We have to point out to Bruner that *abusus non tollit usum*, abuse does not abolish right use. Jesus no more forswears the use of the power that his Father has given him, on the ground that it could be used wrongly and become an instrument in the enemy's hand, than Paul forswears the gift of tongues because it had become an instrument of the self-assertion and unlovingness of the Corinthians. In both cases, the answer to the perversion of wrong use is restoration to right use.

In the current charismatic renewal there has undoubtedly been immature self-indulgence and seeking of superior status in some who have claimed the blessings of the Holy Spirit, but a collection of the stories of disaster that have followed can do no more than warn us that there are dangerous temptations for all who travel in these paths. They provide no excuse at all for retreating from this whole matter back into some supposedly 'safe' church tradition, from which the whole charismatic dimension has been excluded.

It was at any rate not excluded from the ministry of Jesus. When he refused signs, it was because he heard again in those who asked for them, the same voice of unbelief that he had heard in the wilderness. People again tried to implicate him in putting God to the test, because they refused to believe the word that God had already given them in his speaking and acting.

Mark 8:11–12 is typical of those passages in which Jesus refuses a sign, "The Pharisees came and began to argue with him, seeking from him a sign from heaven, to test him. And he sighed deeply in his spirit (*pneuma*) and said, 'Why does this generation seek a sign? Truly I say to you, no sign shall be given to this generation.' " It is consistent with the decision taken in the wilderness that amidst the arguments and traps of arrogant unbelief, no sign is to be given.

But contrast with this the very different reply to the question of John the Baptist, who comes with a question that springs from doubt that is open rather than unbelief which is closed. "Go and tell John what you hear and see: the blind receive their sight and the lame walk, lepers are cleansed and the deaf hear, and the dead are raised up, and the poor have good news preached to them. And blessed is he who takes no offence at me" (Matt. 11:4–6).

To the man who has eyes to see and a faith to understand, Jesus shows the signs of the kingdom in terms of outward manifestation—"What you hear and see". He sends back to John the good news that God is working and ruling not just inwardly and secretly, but in every realm of human need and bondage, so that his Messiahship is certified by the kind of ministry he is exercising and the kind of results that are proceeding from it.

"But if it is by the Spirit of God that I cast out demons, then the kingdom of God has come upon you" (Matt. 12:28). The manifestation of the power of the Spirit in the mighty works of Jesus always stops short of compelling proof. The boundary between this age, which is the age of faith, and the age to come, which is the age of sight, is always respected. The sign given is always sufficiently ambiguous to leave room for the decision of faith. It is quite possible for the hostile Pharisees to give his work a completely different interpretation from his own, "It is only by Beelzebub, the prince of demons that this man casts out demons" (Matt. 12:24). The sign given, the exorcism performed, points with all the logic of faith towards the interpretation that it is a work of the Spirit, but unbelief cannot follow that logic, and is left room to misinterpret the sign within its own presuppositions.

The sign does not dictate the decision of faith, but it urgently requires that a decision should, one way or the other, be taken, and that commitment for or against Jesus should be made. The deed done, added to the word spoken, poses the question about Jesus with an urgency that demands answer. The deed done requires us to say whether he who performed it is an instrument of Beelzebub or an agent of God.

We are not therefore to be surprised if all contemporary manifestations of the Spirit carry with them the same ambiguity and are open to a whole variety of competing interpretations. It is still possible to regard them as natural coincidences ("The crowd said that it had thundered." John 12:29), or psychical curiosities ("Others said 'An angel has spoken to him' "). Jesus manifests the Father's glory in a way that can be seen and heard, but only, as he often said, for those who had ears to hear and eyes to see. His mighty works, then and now, both create faith and build up opposition, but they bring the gospel back out of the realm of irrelevant verbalisation into the realm of contemporary relevant action and compel people to say where they stand in regard to it.

After Jesus's sermon at Nazareth little is said of the Holy Spirit in the gospel narrative. We have already indicated the reasons for this; John Taylor reminds us of the chief of them. "It is because Christ's mode of relationship with him (the Spirit) must always be understood as the characteristic *par excellence* of the new age that we find only a handful of explicit references to the Holy Spirit in the synoptic gospels apart from the birth and the baptism ... [This] is entirely typical of the great reserve that characterises all Jesus' teaching about himself and his role in the popular expectations of the messianic age. The sparseness of the statements about the Spirit corresponds with the fact that the title *Christos* or Messiah occurs only 53 times in the four gospels ... whereas we find it 280 times in the rest of the New Testament." (5) In other words Jesus did not speak of the Spirit, because the Spirit could not then be spoken of, but the presence and power of the Spirit are present in all his words and actions. Consider the following:

(a) The activity of the Spirit is evidenced by the fact that his words and deeds were performed with God-given authority. A typical comment on the early ministry of Jesus is that "they were astonished at his teaching, for his word was with authority" (*exousia*) (Luke 4:32). So also of his works "With authority (*exousia*) he commands the unclean spirits, and they obey him" (Mark 1:27). And the same idea expressed without the use of the word, "And the men marvelled saying, 'What sort of a man is this that even winds and sea obey him'" (Matt. 8:27). As well as the lives of men, the secrets of the supernatural and the elements of nature are subject to his power.

In this context the word authority is very strong indeed—it means a God-given right and power to effect that which he commands. His words were characterised not merely by their intellectual validity and truth-content, but even more by the power that was in him to make happen that which he said. This is the characteristic of the divine word (*dabar*) in the Old Testament, "And God said, 'Let there be light' and there was light" (Gen. 1:3). The word of Jesus operates in precisely the same way, "He said to the paralytic, 'I say to you, rise, take up your pallet, and go home'. And he rose and immediately took up the pallet and went out before them all; so that they were all amazed and glorified God, saying "we never saw anything like this" (Mark 2:10-12). This visible happening was, in the context of the narrative, the outward sign of the invisible event of the forgiveness of sins which (v. 5) his word had effected with the same authority.

Precisely this connection between the authoritative word spoken and the visible event that results from it is evidenced again and again as characteristic of the ministry of the Holy Spirit in the New Testament Church. Paul describes it thus, "My speech and my message were not in plausible words of wisdom, but in demonstration of the Spirit and power" (1 Cor. 2:4). This powerful activity of the Spirit accompanied the ministry of Paul because first it was typical of the ministry of Jesus.

(b) There appear in the ministry of Jesus, many of the *charismata*, later to be identified as such in the Church. The word of wisdom with which he dealt with those who wanted to trap him with the Roman coin (Mark 12:13–17), the word of knowledge with which he told the woman at the well "all that she ever did" (John 4:29), the acts of power (*dunamis*) he performed, the faith with which he moved mountains of impossibility, the prophetic voice with which he unfolded her fate to Jerusalem, the healings with which his ministry abounded—all show that the *charismata* Paul lists in 1 Corinthians 12:8–11, are by no means innovations, but go back to the archetypal work of the same Spirit in the ministry of Jesus, so that they have Christological grounding in the work of the Spirit in his humanity, before they appear in ours. Special questions arise here about the relationship of the gift of tongues to the ministry of Jesus, and we shall be discussing these in an appendix to chapter nine, but meantime the general statement stands, that the *charismata* of the Church are firmly grounded in the ministry of the Lord.

Jesus' ministry has often been expounded in terms of the truth he taught and the compassion he showed. But inextricably bound up with these is the specifically charismatic dimension. He taught and he loved, with power and with authority to change people and things, and to do for them, and make happen in them, what his word declared and his love desired. There is no need to set up any opposition between the gospel as declaration of truth, service of love, act of power. Power outside the context of love and truth is precisely that to which the enemy tempted Jesus in the wilderness, and to which for example the Church in Corinth is tempted again so that it has to be reminded that *charismata* exercised outside the context of love are worth nothing at all (1 Cor. 13). So a seeking of charismatic power outside the context of the truth of the gospel is irresponsible and dangerous.

But a truth that is only intellectual and objective, and a love that is only a moral quality and that does not have the power and the means to effect that which it longs for—these are not the truth or the love of which the New Testament speaks. The Spirit who authenticates the truth and matures the love, also provides the power for both to move into action, and, in the charismatic enactment of the truth, to manifest the present glory of God's mighty love. It is that enacted truth which the world waits to see in the Church.

The whole thrust of our argument insists that this gift of spiritual authority and effectiveness, which characterises the ministry of Jesus and points to the activity of the Spirit in it, is by no means confined to that ministry. This was not the exclusive prerogative of the Son of God. He poured out the power of the Spirit on his own humanity in order that by the same Spirit it should be conveyed to ours.

The promise of John 14:12 to this effect we have already quoted. But even before Pentecost, and within the Gospels it is made clear that the authority of Jesus can be shared, and that authority to proclaim and to perform are one and the same. "And he called the twelve and gave them power and authority (*dunamin kai exousian*) over all demons and to cure diseases; and he sent them out to preach the kingdom of God and to heal" (Luke 9:1–2). Even within the Gospels there is this preliminary impartation of the authority of the Spirit that had worked till now exclusively in Jesus, to his disciples so that it may work through them.

At Pentecost that becomes general and abiding. The ministry of Christ in Galilee is continued in his people. It is not merely a unique episode to be looked back at; it prefigures the outpouring of the Spirit in power upon the whole Church in order that by the same mighty deeds and words it may manifest its Lord's glory in the world. A gospel that remains in the realm of intellectual orthodoxy or humanistic compassion cannot but fail to grasp the dynamism of the Holy Spirit to come and by his mighty acts realise the kingdom again among us.

The flesh and the devil would divert God's people into lack of appropriation, or misappropriation, of the power and the gifts of the Spirit, but the Spirit of Christ strives against the flesh and resists the devil, and empowers us to manifest the kingdom both in the kind of people we are and the kinds of works that we do, so that the truth, love, power of Christ may in their oneness appear in us, to the glory of the Father.

NOTES

1 Karl Barth, *Church Dogmatics*, IV. 1, p. 261
2 Anders Nygren, *Commentary on Romans* (S.C.M.), p. 315
3 Edward Irving, *The Orthodox and Catholic Doctrine of our Lord's Human Nature* (London 1830) pp. vii–viii
4 F. D. Bruner, *A Theology of the Holy Spirit* (Hodder & Stoughton), (S.C.M.), p. 224
5 John Taylor, *The Go-Between God* (S.C.M.), pp. 86–7

CHAPTER EIGHT

Cross and Spirit

WE HAVE looked at the work of the Spirit in initiating Jesus into his ministry by birth and baptism, and in the midst of his ministry in the years in Galilee, and now we are to look at the relationship of the Spirit to the crown and completion of his ministry in the cross and resurrection.

Where this relationship has not been recognised and grasped, people have understandably felt uncomfortable about the claims of the charismatic renewal. They rightly judge that anything, however experientially exciting, however edifying the gifts that it may have brought to light, which is not centrally anchored in Calvary and Easter is suspect in the extreme, and might well prove little more than a distraction and diversion from the main Christian concern with the crucified and risen Lord. Those who owe most to the evangelical tradition continually raise questions about how this new emphasis on the Spirit is connected with the Saviourhood of Jesus, and some go as far as to suggest that to speak at all of a renewing work of the Spirit is to derogate from the completeness of Christ's finished work, and to suggest that it needs augmentation and supplementation.

It is obvious that where this kind of thing is said, the second blessing theory of the Baptism in the Holy Spirit is still exercising

104

its baneful influence; people are still thinking of salvation in Christ and the blessing of the Spirit as two separate gifts of God, each in its way requiring the other; neither able to make a claim to completeness without the other; and thus in latent competition with each other.

We have already made clear our attitude to such a view and need not repeat it. A Spirit who could derogate from the glory of Christ crucified in order to promote a more dazzling glory of his own, who passes by the sufferings of Christ in order to offer us a share in a painless and costless triumph, is certainly not the Holy Spirit of the New Testament. He glorifies, not himself, but Christ, and therefore his mission is to reveal the full glory of Calvary, and to bring us into possession of all the blessings that by his death Christ has won for us. Here also the work of the Spirit is to take the things of Christ and show them to us, so that, in the way appropriate to us, we may reflect his glory and be shaped into his likeness.

This was brought home to me very memorably, when a few months after I had entered into a new experience of this Spirit, I went to my first neo-Pentecostalist conference organised by the late Dr. D. P. Thomson, then of St. Ninian's, Crieff, who had the prophetic discernment to see that something major had begun to move in the churches. There for the first time I dared to speak in tongues in public, and the interpretation was given by a young woman, unknown to me before or since, who said, "There is no way to Pentecost except by Calvary; the Spirit is given from the cross." I was deeply impressed by that at the time and have tried to let it become one of the main themes in my teaching about the Spirit ever since. In passing, the whole incident perhaps provides a minor illustration of how even the gift of tongues can find its own Christological significance!

The dependence of Pentecost on Calvary will in fact be the subject of the first major section of this chapter; we shall try to show how the Spirit proceeds from the cross; then in the second section, we shall make the complementary emphasis, that the

Spirit leads us to the cross, and in this double way we shall try to describe the relationship between the two.

1 That Pentecost is a consequence of Calvary is in fact a New Testament theme, sounded most often and most clearly in St. John's Gospel, and there always by way of simple statement or allusion, rather than by any kind of theological explanation.

The whole subject comes to expression first in John 7:37-39. After reporting the call of Jesus to the thirsty to come and drink, and the promise that those who believe in him will have rivers of living water flow from their inmost being, the author breaks in with a remarkable editorial insertion, in which he seems to futurise and relocate the promise he has just reported, by explaining that its fulfilment belongs not to the ministry of Christ in Judaea, but rather to the ministry of the ascended Lord, "Now this he said about the Spirit, which those who believed in him were going to receive (*emellon lambanein*); for as yet the Spirit had not been given (*oupo gar en pneuma*) because Jesus was not yet glorified (*oudepo edoxasthe*)." The pouring out of the Spirit upon and from believers is consequent upon that event which John describes here as the glorification of Jesus, and elsewhere as his going away (*apelthein*, John 16:7) or his being lifted up (*hupsothenai*—John 3:14; 12:32, 34). All three terms refer to the whole series of events —cross, Easter, ascension, his being lifted up on the cross to die, his being lifted up from the grave to live, his being lifted up to the Father to reign—and it is upon the completion of that series of events that the release of the Spirit depends.

John 16:7 says the same thing more explicitly. "It is to your advantage that I go away, for if I do not go away the Counsellor will not come to you (*ou me*, emphatic negative almost = 'cannot come'); but if I go, I will send him to you." Here the fruit of the cross is seen to be the coming of the Spirit. That coming, far from being in competition with Calvary, is in fact a consequence of it. The New Testament never confines the benefits of Christ's death to the abolition of the bad past and the securing of the eternal future—to the forgiveness of sins by his blood. The right relationship with God that his death establishes is by no means a formal or empty relationship. God justifies us for a purpose, and that purpose is that the likeness of Christ should by the outpouring of the Paraclete be formed in us.

Thus the charismatic renewal, if it understands itself aright, is not deflecting or distracting attention from the death of Christ. It is simply saying that among the 'all things' that God gave us with him when he delivered him up for us all (Rom. 8:32) there is the experience of the Spirit's fullness and the ability to share in and serve by his power and gifts. The "magnificently varied grace of God" (*poikile charis*) of 1 Peter 4:10 (J. B. Phillips), which has reached us through Christ's death, also contains the concrete *charismata* which are being rediscovered.

He died not just "that we might be forgiven" (our justification), not just "to make us good" (our sanctification), not just "that we might go at last to heaven" (our salvation), but that, in and with all these we might in our new humanity be called and equipped to take up his mission and to be witnesses to the drawing near of his kingdom. For this also, it was to our advantage that he should go away.

The same connection is forged in the specific context of the day of Pentecost in our key verse Acts 2:33, where Christ's exaltation to the right hand of God, consequent upon his death and resurrection, is interpreted as involving "Having received from the Father the promise of the Holy Spirit," as a result of which he pours out all the visible and audible things that have happened that day. This promise of the Holy Spirit which he received from the Father is probably not personal to Christ (that had been fulfilled in his own manhood and for his own mission at his baptism), but rather the promise he made to his people and which can now be fulfilled as he presents himself to the Father as the crucified and risen one. Again the coming of the Spirit is the consequence of the going away of Jesus.

To return to John, as he inserts his theology of the cross into his account of Calvary, so in the same account he suggests more than once the connection between the finished work of Jesus and the coming of the Spirit. Having in 19:30 recorded the great triumphant *Tetelestai*, "It is finished," John goes on to tell us how Jesus bowed his head and, in the Greek, *paredoken to pneuma*. The obvious English translation is "he gave up the ghost" (A.V.), or even "he died". Hoskyns and Davey comment, "The Johannine record maybe so phrased as to describe the voluntary death of the Christ, and may have no further significance. But it is very strange language." (1) The verb used (*paradidomi*) means to pass on a tradition from hand to hand. It is in fact used in the introductory words of the institution of the Lord's Supper in 1 Corinthians 11:23, "I received from the Lord what I delivered (*paredoka*) to you," so that a literal translation of the last words of John 19:30 would be, "He handed over, traditioned the Spirit." To quote Hoskyns and Davey again, "If it be assumed that the author intends his readers to suppose that the Beloved Disciple and Mary the Mother of Jesus remain standing beneath the cross, the words 'he bowed his head' suggest that he bowed his head towards them and the words 'he handed over the Spirit' is also directed to the faithful believers who stand below." (2)

The same authors point to the close connection between this verse and the piercing with the spear that follows, and how taken together they fulfil John 7:37-39. Now Jesus is glorified and the promise he has made to others is immediately fulfilled in himself, because out of his belly (*koilia*), pierced by the soldier's spear, there flow rivers of living water, and the water and the Spirit are one.

This leads us on to claim John 19:34 as a further Johannine indication of the gift of the Spirit from the cross, "But one of the soldiers pierced his side with a spear, and at once there came out blood and water." There is no need to deny a sacramental interpretation in order to establish a spiritual one, that is, one referring to the work and gift of the Spirit. To say that John sees the two sacraments as established in the death of Christ is only another way of saying that the Spirit is released from the cross.

Just as blood is particularly associated with the forgiveness of sins, so water is particularly associated with the gift of the Spirit.

By water and the Spirit our Christian initiation is achieved (John 3:5), by water that stands for the Spirit thirst is assuaged so that the water that Christ gives us becomes in us springs of water welling up to eternal life (John 4:14), and by the water of the Spirit that flows from us we are constituted as Christ's witnesses to the world (John 7:38).

That water and that blood and that Spirit alike and together flow from Calvary and bear witness to all that the Lord has done there. So 1 John 5:8, "There are three witnesses, the Spirit and the the water and the blood: and these three agree."

It is significant that in the Johannine anticipation of Pentecost (John 20:19-23), it is the risen Christ who has identified himself with the crucified Jesus by showing his disciples his hands and his side (John 20:20), who summons them afresh to their missionary calling, "As the Father has sent me, even so I send you" (John 20:21), and in that context breathes upon them the Spirit and says, "Receive the Holy Spirit" (John 20:22).

I cannot agree with those who, in a desire to differentiate between this bestowal of the Spirit and the day of Pentecost, refer what happens here to regeneration. It seems to me quite clear from the context that this passage as much as Acts 2 has to do with the giving of authority for mission and witness, an authority in John more closely identified with the inner work of forgiveness, and in Acts more with outward manifestation.

If the accurate tracing of the historical sequence is all that is important to us, we may perhaps conclude that in John 20 we are still in the realm of promise, but of promise so close to its fulfilment that it can actually in retrospect be presented as being already fulfilled on Easter evening, whereas the actual historical breakthrough of the Spirit into experience and in power was on the day of Pentecost.

But infinitely more important than the historical harmonisation of the two accounts is their basic theological agreement that, however and whenever the Spirit was given, he was given to the disciples for the fulfilment of their calling, and he was given by the one who had died on the cross and had risen from the dead. Although the experiential participation in the blessing was delayed until Pentecost, the objective procuring of the gift was included, as surely as the forgiveness of sins, in the finished work of the cross.

To move on to Paul, the relationship between cross and Spirit is indicated clearly in Galatians 3 where the series of questions at the beginning of the Chapter clearly establish that it was the public portrayal of Christ crucified before their eyes (v. 1), actualised in their hearing the gospel with faith (v. 2) that resulted in such a receiving of the Spirit (v. 3) as led to outstanding experiences (v. 4), to a constant supply of the Spirit and God's working of miracles among them (v. 5). This passage in fact contains the full description of a New Testament conversion, or initiation in Christ. It begins with a proclamation of the cross and advances to an outpouring of the Spirit in all his experienced reality and power—and any offer of conversion which holds out less than that fails to do justice to the full extent of what is available to us in Christ crucified.

Paul formulates the principle involved further on in the same chapter when he says, "Christ redeemed us from the curse of the law, having become a curse for us—for it is written, 'Cursed be everyone who hangs upon a tree'—that in Christ Jesus the blessing of Abraham might come upon the Gentiles, that we might receive the promise of the Spirit through faith" (Gal. 3:13–14).

Thus there is a necessary connection between the release of the Spirit and the bearing of the consequences of sin. Only after the Son of God has achieved reconciliation for our sinful humanity, by bearing in it the death which is the wages of sin, and by offering to God the perfect obedience that he requires, can right relationships be established between God and our humanity. But when the passive obedience of atoning suffering, and the active obedience of perfect response to the Father have been offered vicariously and representatively for us by Christ in the midst of our humanity, the Spirit who dwelt and worked freely in him can come to dwell and work freely in us.

In our unreconciled state the Spirit cannot come. The judgment of God, on the one side, and the reign of sin on the other, stand between us and him. But Christ takes our flesh into union with himself and bears in it the judgment of God that was its due, thus fulfilling on Calvary that identification with sinners that began in his baptism. By the Holy Spirit he breaks the reign of sin in our flesh, that tried to entrap him at his temptations, so that on Calvary a perfect human life is offered in a perfect sacrifice. Thus on the basis of Christ's work, we are able to participate in his reconciled manhood and the Spirit who dwells in him comes to dwell in us.

To say the same thing in terms of Romans 8, God has sent his own Son in a real sharing of our sinful flesh and he has condemned sin in the flesh (v. 3) that is, borne its judgment and broken its power. As a result the law is fulfilled as far as we are concerned (v. 4) and we may now walk in the Spirit (v. 4), enjoy the status of sonship (v. 16), and enter as joint heirs into that spiritual inheritance which we see in him and which in the Spirit can be ours (v. 17).

Professor T. F. Torrance has given all this memorable expression as follows:

> It was only at infinite cost that Jesus Christ gained for us the gift of the Holy Spirit, receiving him in all his consuming holiness into the human nature which he took from our fallen and alienated condition ... Until he had sanctified himself and perfected in our human nature his one offering for all men, until he had made the once and for all sacrifice to take away sin, until he had vanquished the powers of darkness and overcome the sharpness of death, until he had ascended to present himself in propitiation before the Father, the kingdom of heaven could not be opened to believers, and the blessing of the divine Spirit could not be poured out upon human flesh or be received by sinful mortal men. (3)

In the light of all this it is not surprising that on the day of Pentecost Peter offers the Jerusalem crowd the twin blessings of the forgiveness of sins and the gifts of the Holy Spirit, released in fullness (Acts 2:38). Both equally are the fruits of Calvary, the gifts of the Crucified, and where the gift of the Spirit is supplanted in faith or experience by a onesided emphasis on the forgiveness of sins, the full fruits of Calvary are left unplucked and untasted. There can be no conflict between the gospel of the cross and the gift of the Spirit. The Spirit glorifies Christ crucified by exhibiting to us, and then in us, the full inheritance of the sons of God he died to make us.

2   But the doctrine of the cross in the New Testament has another aspect to which so far we have not alluded. Not only is the cross that which uniquely he bears for us, for our atonement and reconciliation, but it is also the ruling principle of the Christian life. As atonement was made through a cross where the Man suffered, so witness to that atonement can be made only by witnesses who exhibit the reality of that to which they witness in their own suffering. We have only to retranslate a single word of Acts 1:8 to make that clear and to bring the whole verse into a completely fresh perspective, "You shall be martyrs—suffering witnesses (*martureis*)—to me."

The Holy Spirit's function is to reflect in us the likeness of Christ—of his truth and love and power—but how could he do that with any authenticity or completeness, if he did not also lead us into the likeness of his suffering? There could be no real reflection of Christ that did not consist of bearing his cross.

The Holy Spirit, far from being the promoter or guarantee of any kind of costless triumphalism, is in the New Testament always the Spirit who leads to sacrifice. This is true first in the experience of Jesus. We have seen already how his baptismal initiation was at the same time a prefiguration of Calvary and a foretaste of Pentecost; the two elements were present together from the very first, he was endued with power, and he was marked for sacrifice. It was because the Spirit of the Lord was upon him that he went to Calvary. This is true both of the outward development and of the inner necessity of his ministry.

When we were discussing the authority of Jesus' words and deeds, we stressed that, while they by no means compelled faith, they did demand decision and revealed the issues involved so sharply that they led people to a critical parting of the ways, where they were forced to commitment either for or against Jesus. It is sometimes said that the charismatic renewal is divisive and we have seen how it can be, in a wrong way, that springs from the pride and prejudices of men. But it is still true that the first charismatic renewal when the Man filled with the Spirit was set loose in mighty word and deed throughout Galilee, was inevitably and deeply divisive. By its sheer reality and authenticity, by its bringing the issue of the kingdom out of their theological remoteness and manifesting the glory of God in deeds done to neighbours on the lakeside and in the market place, a situation was created where neutrality towards it became impossible. Religious men were exposed and troubled by the present power of what had so long been safely cocooned in intellectual theory and pious practice, that they had either to surrender to it or fight it to the death. In the outward development of the ministry of Jesus, it was the hostile reaction of the Jewish ecclesiastical authorities to the manifestation of the Holy Spirit in his ministry, that sent him to the cross.

To be filled with the Spirit is not to discover an easy way to win friends and influence people. Revival movements have always aroused criticism and rejection within the communities where they started. Some of that criticism is no doubt their own fault, but that is not the whole story. As long as the Church talks piously within its own walls, it can be ignored and tolerated. But where Christians begin to come even a little into the authentic likeness of their master, then, as he promised, they will be hated as he was hated and rejected as he was rejected. There are many in the world, and also in the Church who will be stung into the self-defence of rejecting opposition by the appearance of the signs of Christ's presence and power.

As with the Master, so with the disciples. Peter and John and the rest would have been left untroubled in their upper room, if they had stayed quiet with their memories, but when the Spirit came upon them, the boldness (*parrhesia*) of their words and deeds challenged the Jewish authorities in the same way that Jesus had challenged them and soon had them in prison. Wherever Paul went, as someone has put it, there was both riot and revival, and he was as much the victim of the former as he was promoter of the latter. The power of God let loose among the people of God again and again brought them to lift up their own cross and follow Christ.

But if it was the manifested power of the Spirit that outwardly provoked Jesus' death, it was the same Spirit who inwardly motivated him to Calvary. It is the Holy Spirit who opens Jesus' eyes to the fulfilment of his baptismal identification with sinners in his atoning death. He who saw the anointing of the Spirit as his enablement for his mission to open blind eyes and bring good news to the poor and release to the prisoners, is progressively led to see that he can fulfil his mission only by identifying himself with the suffering Servant of Isaiah 53 and by giving his life as a ransom for many. Only thus can he fully manifest his Father's glory, for which the blessing of the Spirit was given.

This inner connection between the work of the Spirit and the offering of blood is established in Hebrews 9:14, "How much more shall the blood of Christ, who *through the eternal Spirit offered himself* without blemish to God, purify your conscience from dead works to serve the living God."

In delicate exegesis of this unexplained hint we cannot do better than quote John Taylor,

What was the Holy Spirit doing at Calvary? First, in a mystery that we cannot plumb, he must have been about his eternal employ between the Father and the Son, holding each in awareness of the other, in an agony of bliss and love that must for ever lie infinitely beyond our understanding. For Jesus this included both the forsakenness and the ultimate trust . . . But, beyond the inwardness of the Trinity, the Spirit of communion spilled out into other awareness; his concern for others, surpassing the pain, and their deepening perception of him. The thief's and the centurion's recognition . . . was the start of a turning of eyes that has been going on ever since. (4)

The Holy Spirit at the heart of the cross is the Spirit of sacrifice; the Christ who at his baptism chose to be the servant of sinners as he received the Spirit, who in his ministry used his powers to give himself without measure to others, in his dying gave himself 'through the eternal Spirit' for others to his Father.

To call him the Spirit of sacrifice is to call him the Spirit of love, of Christ's kind of self-giving love, communicated by the Spirit from him to us. Romans 5:5 speaks of how "God's love has been poured into our hearts through the Holy Spirit which has been given to us," and goes on to expound the nature of that love in terms of the cross. "But God shows his love for us in that while we were yet sinners Christ died for us" (v. 8). That love was definitely and ultimately expressed on Calvary, and from Calvary the Spirit brings it to us, and in leading us to share his powerful active self-giving to and for the unworthy, the Spirit forms us in his likeness.

The mark of the cross rests upon every expression of the Holy Spirit's activity. With Jesus, the Spirit-filled man and community has been turned from itself to give itself first to God and then to others both inside and outside the fellowship. The fruit of the Spirit has grown and ripened on the tree at Golgotha. The *koinonia*, fellowship of the Spirit, which is the primary expression of the Church's life and mission, is only possible when people have learnt to sacrifice, to yield the flesh to be crucified in order that we may be ligaments in the Body of Christ.

The gifts of the Spirit are the gifts of the crucified. To be involved in the ministry of healing and identify with people who are facing the mystery of their sickness and of God's grace in it, is to taste a little of Calvary. To be a fool for Christ and to know the loneliness of the prophet is to carry a little cross that is the same shape as his great one. To be in the Spirit is to be brought again and again to the point where all human self-sufficiency has to die, and the only answer is a miracle of resurrection. It is when the Church comes to that point, that she can begin to be renewed.

To know anything of life in the Spirit is to know that it is never any kind of frothy instant-answer triumphalism; it has its dark mysteries as well as its glorious ministries. It conforms us to Christ both in his suffering and his triumph. The more we know of the power of the Spirit, the more we shall also know of the experience of the cross.

Within the New Testament the pre-eminent example of all this is Stephen, who is twice said to be "a man full of faith and of the Holy Spirit" and "full of grace and power" (Acts 6:5, 8). By the very boldness of his speech he brought opposition upon himself, "They could not withstand the wisdom and the Spirit with which he spoke" (Acts 6:10).

But in his death Stephen attained the most remarkable likeness and reflection of his master. He knew the love of Jesus in all its forgiving generosity, "Lord, do not hold this sin against them" (Acts 7:60), and the trust of Jesus at his own death, "Lord Jesus, receive my spirit" (Acts 7:59). That is life—and death—in the fullness of the Spirit, and so in the fullness of Christ and his sacrifice.

And like the death of Christ, such death is never fruitless or vain. Keeping the clothes as they stoned Stephen was a young man called Saul, and the pricks that pressed on the road to Damascus were his memories of Stephen, so that the fruit of the death in the Spirit of the great martyr was the birth in the Spirit of the great apostle.

The principle of Stephen's martyrdom has its classic statement within the New Testament in Philippians 3:10, "That I may know him, and the power (*dunamis*) of his resurrection, and the fellowship (*koinonia*) of his sufferings". The order, in contrast to that of the second half of the verse, is unexpected and deliberate. It is the man who in the Spirit knows the power of Christ's resurrection, the renewing power that came upon the Lord at Jordan and the apostles at Pentecost, who will also, as a result of what has come upon him, enter into the fellowship of Christ's sufferings. And we need both; the power of the Spirit by itself would spoil us, but to keep us with Paul from being too much exalted (II Cor. 12:7) we are given a share of the cross, which by itself would break us. In that constant alternating current of spiritual electricity, by which first Christ gives freely to us and then freely we pour ourselves out for him, we live our life in the mystery of the resurrection—cross-resurrection, suffering that begets joy, and power that leads to pain.

The Spirit who comes to us through the Son from the Father as the Spirit of Pentecost is the same Spirit by whom through the Son we offer ourselves in sacrifice to the Father. T. F. Torrance has recently pointed out that the Pentecostal emphasis on the Spirit as the one we receive, needs to be integrated with the Catholic emphasis on the Spirit as the one who identifies us with Christ in his sacrifice,

> The fact that the historical Catholic Churches of East and West have been taking a great interest in the recent movements of the Spirit, would also seem to indicate the shape of things ahead; the characteristic Catholic emphasis, in the Spirit, through the Son to the Father, and the characteristic Pentecostalist emphasis, from the Father, through the Son in the Spirit, would then be brought together again. (5)

We have seen that the Spirit *comes from* the cross, as a result of the work done there, and *leads* us *to* the cross, in identification with the sacrifice offered there. The Spirit is the Spirit of Calvary and the authenticating sign of his working in our lives is the appearance of the spiritual stigmata, the identifying marks of the cross.

NOTES

1   Sir Edwyn Hoskyns, edited by F. N. Davey, *The Fourth Gospel* (Faber and Faber), p. 532
2   Ibid.
3   T. F. Torrance, *Theology in Reconstruction* (S.C.M.), p. 248
4   John Taylor, *The Go-Between God* (S.C.M.), p. 102
5   T. F. Torrance, 'The Church in the New Era of Scientific and Cosmological Change', in New College, Edinburgh, *Bulletin* 1973, p. 31

CHAPTER NINE

His Lifegiving Body

BY RESURRECTION and ascension, Christ, the new man, comes at last into his own. The days of his 'trials' have ended on Calvary, and he now enters into the kingdom his Father has appointed for him (Luke 22:28). In our flesh, in our circumstances, in our stead, he has done bitter battle with the world, the flesh and the devil, all the way from the beginning in Bethlehem to the climax on the cross and now, by bearing the judgment due to sin and by offering a complete obedience, he has made our humanity in himself open completely to the Holy Spirit, and has been exalted to the place of all power with the Father, so that he may pour out his Spirit upon all flesh.

As we examine the complex event of Easter-ascension-Pentecost, we see again the emergence of the themes that have dominated our understanding of his whole life and ministry—the renewal of manhood in him by the Holy Spirit, and the reflection of that renewed manhood in us by the coming of the same Spirit.

Commenting on Romans 1:4, Leehardt writes, "The Resurrection has inaugurated first for him, then for believers a new era; the Christ has been designated Son of God in power by the fact that his resurrection has brought into being the age of the Spirit, according to ancient prophecy." (1)

Paul relates the new era of the Spirit to the resurrection of Jesus in more than one passage. In Ephesians 1:19-20, he connects the power at work in believers with the energy that raised Christ from the dead, and says that the latter is the norm and source of the former, describing "what is the immeasurable greatness of his power in us who believe, according to the working of his great might which he accomplished in Christ, when he raised him from the dead and made him sit at his right hand in the heavenly places".

In Romans 8:11, which we have already discussed, the Spirit is shown to be the agent both of Christ's resurrection and of the new life of believers and its manifestations in their body. "If the Spirit of him who raised Christ Jesus from the dead dwells in you, he who raised Christ Jesus from the dead will give life to your mortal bodies also through his Spirit that dwells in you."

This presentation of the risen Christ as the bearer and dispenser of the new spiritual humanity is particularly clear in 1 Corinthians 15 and especially in v. 45, "Thus it is written, 'The first man Adam became a living being' (*psuche zosa*), the last Adam (*eschatos Adam*) became a life-giving Spirit (*pneuma zoopoioun*)." The difference between the two is (a) that the first Adam has natural life (*psuche*) but the last Adam has resurrection life, spiritual life (*pneuma*), and (b) the first Adam has that life only for himself, he is living; whereas the last Adam not only has life, but is a creative source of life for others, and supplies to others that *pneuma* which is the basis of his own being.

James Dunn has most helpfully pointed out that the simple phrase 'life-giving Spirit' (*pneuma zoopoioun*) speaks volumes about the living Christian experience of the Christians to whom it was addressed. He writes,

> *Pneuma zoopoioun*, life-giving Spirit, cannot be understood except as a reference to the spiritual experience of the early believers ... Paul identifies the risen Jesus with this life-giving Spirit; Jesus himself is the source of these experiences of Spirit, or to put it the other way, the experience of life-giving Spirit is experience of the risen Jesus. Moreover, and this is the crucial

point, this experience constitutes for Paul proof that Jesus is risen from the dead. (2)

Paul makes it clear that the spiritual life which the risen Christ imparts is not to be understood in some docetic or hyper-spiritual way, when in v. 44, describing the coming resurrection of believers, in close analogy with the completed resurrection of Christ, he says, "It is sown a physical body (*soma psuchikon*), it is raised a spiritual body (*soma pneumatikon*)." This is based on an understanding of the change which death and resurrection have wrought in Christ's body. He dies in a body which is subject to the physical limitations and laws of the fallen creation, but now, in his resurrection, his body, in which the Spirit manifested himself, has become completely plastic to the operations of the Spirit, has become "spiritual", *pneumatikon*, restored to the incorruptibility and immortality which were God's original design for it.

But within this change the constant factor is *soma*, body—the basic structure of our humanity which gives Christ identity with us at every stage. When he becomes spiritual, he does not cease to be bodily. The resurrection is not the undoing of our humanity, it is its completion and glorification. Christ is *eschatos Adam*, the ultimate Man, and he has been made so by the complete permeation of his body with Spirit.

This is in complete agreement with the gospel accounts of the resurrection, which presumably reflect the same traditions that are at the basis of Paul's teaching in 1 Corinthians 15. There is obviously a difference in the mode of being of the risen Jesus, which the word *pneumatikos*, spiritual, precisely describes. He is no longer recognisable except as he reveals himself, and is not subject to physical limitations, but can come and go in a way that demonstrates his lordship over the physical conditions of his life.

But he remains *somatikos*, embodied. Amidst all the difference there is the continuing human identity between the crucified and the risen Lord, which the gospels again and again go out of their way to emphasise.

Luke 24:36 is typical,

> Jesus himself stood among them. But they were startled and frightened, and supposed that they saw a spirit (*pneuma*). And he said to them, 'Why are you troubled and why do questionings rise in your hearts? See my hands and my feet, that it is I myself; handle me and see; for a spirit (pneuma) has not flesh and bones as you see that I have . . . Have you anything more to eat?' They gave him a piece of broiled fish, and he took it and ate it before them.

The *pneuma* in the risen Jesus is *pneuma somatikon* not ethereal emanation, but the Spirit-filled man brought to the perfection of his humanity. Far from being a later 'materialising accretion' to the narrative, as many commentators wishing to spiritualise the resurrection stories, have made out, this passage in Luke and its parallels are in line with the insight which we have pursued throughout, that the concern of the Spirit, especially when he is acting in his resurrection power, is the re-creation of man in all his totality. There was an *empty* tomb on Easter morning; the whole man was raised, his whole body and spirit had become the place of operation of the Holy Spirit; that risen body of Jesus is the proto-type, glorified but more than ever human, which the Holy Spirit will ultimately copy completely in us.

Just as the miracle of his birth has its physical, gynaecological implications, just as the miracles of his ministry affect sick bodies and loaves of bread and the lake water of Galilee, so the Easter gospel proclaims the rising of the total man in the power of the Spirit, and any spiritualising attack upon any or all of these, with its implied docetic dismissal of whole areas of our humanity from the operation of the Spirit, falls short of the gospel which proclaims that Christ is, by the Spirit, the ultimate Man in which God's creation of our manhood is brought to its glorious goal. Such a charismatic humanism is far nearer the gospel than the hyper-spiritualising that has so often marred interpretations at this point.

Into the image of Christ's spiritual body, as prototype of our resurrected humanity, we are ultimately to be made, as Paul declares in 1 Corinthians 15:49, "Just as we have borne the image of the man of dust, we shall also bear the image (*eikon*) of the man of heaven." This is our common destiny, already reached by the ascended Christ, but still in the realm of hope for Christians.

There is both a 'now' and a 'not yet' about the operation of the Spirit of resurrection in this present age. There is a present sharing in the life power, and glory of the risen Lord (cf II Cor. 3:18, Eph. 1:19–20), we can now share in the power of his resurrection (Phil. 3:10), the Spirit of resurrection can not only dwell in our inmost heart but operate in our mortal bodies also (Rom. 9:11). The eschatological 'there and then' has effectively broken through into the 'here and now', in many forms, and, in particular, through charismatic gifts and ministries, and does so in order to bear witness to the effective present action of that Ultimate Man who keeps on coming, even while we are still waiting for his final coming.

The great gospel commentator Bengal once said of the gospel miracles, "*Spirant resurrectionem*—they breathe resurrection," and this could be said equally of the charismatic gifts and ministries. They are not simply the work of dedicated human talent, they have been given a new and transcendent reference. What happens in them points to the operation, not of natural human forces, but of the power that raised Jesus from the dead.

This is the distinction between healing through the skills and processes of medicine, and spiritual healing in the name of Christ, which, for example, John Taylor (3) seems to me to miss. It is not that one is better or more God-given than the other, it is simply that the witness they bear is different. Medical healing bears witness to the providence of God in creation, providing within the natural order remedies and human skills for the ills of his creatures, whereas divine healing bears witness to the operation of the Holy Spirit breaking through the limitations of the natural in a way analogous to what he did when he raised Christ from the dead.

The one gives testimony to a God who provides within creation, the other gives testimony to a risen Christ and a God who can reverse natural process and raise the dead.

But the 'not-yet' remains. "We ourselves, who have the first-fruits (*aparche*) of the Spirit, groan inwardly as we wait for adoption as sons, the redemption of our bodies" (Rom. 8:23). What we have in the Spirit—the reality of adoption which already lets us cry 'Abba, Father' (Rom. 8:15), the creative touch on our humanity which already brings the new creation to light—makes us long for that which we do not yet have, the full outworking and manifestation of what it means to be God's children, the complete restoration of our humanity in Christ. That remains in the realm of hope, but of realistic hope, because of what has happened already.

The same tension is reflected in Ephesians 1:14 where we are told that we "were sealed with the promised Holy Spirit, which is the first instalment (*arrabon*) of our inheritance, until we acquire possession of it". The *arrabon*, like the *aparche*, is that which is given now, and which is a guaranteeing promise of the much more yet to come.

Within that tension of the already given and the still to come all Christians have to live—including charismatic Christians. God gives enough evidence of Christ risen to call to faith, but not enough to compel to acceptance. Again and again the gifts of the Spirit operate, and yet they are never at our disposal. There remains something sovereign and elusive about their coming and going. In the realm of healing much happens to authenticate Christ's present will and power to heal the otherwise incurable, and yet, often distressingly, enough fails to happen to serve to remind us that we are not yet at the last day, and to leave the mystery of the 'not-yet' all around us.

It can be dangerous to loosen that tension in either direction. To put Christ's resurrection power exclusively into the future, is to make him again utterly remote and withdrawn from us, and to leave us with our own strivings and efforts 'for Christ' and bereft of participation in his gifts to us. On the other hand, to claim that completeness of resurrection is here and now open to us, is to fall into a cruel charismatic triumphalism, which can lead us to refuse to accept our failures, to deceive others, and perhaps ourselves also, into imagining that everything works out immediately and completely for those who are in the Spirit, that all the prophecies are fulfilled and all the sick are healed. We have in fact to live in a far less simple situation than either of these—in which the comfort of the here and now of the Spirit, and the mystery of the not-yet of the Spirit constantly, and in the end creatively, confront us.

Closely connected with Christ's resurrection is his ascension. We can say in terms of his ascension what we have just been saying in terms of his resurrection. The ascension implies both withdrawal and arrival. It implies withdrawal from his disciples, so that 'a cloud took him out of their sight' (Acts 1:9)—a cloud that in scripture stands for God's glory, into which Jesus takes our manhood, and where we cannot yet follow. There is that in Christ which transcends our present experience, entrance into a kingdom whose reality we believe and cannot yet fully experience, "We do not yet see everything in subjection to him" (Heb. 2:8). All power in heaven and on earth is his, but not yet ours. We know our continued identification with him, but it is still a hidden identification, and we long for his appearing, and for our appearing, as we are in him. Thus the ascension does imply the withdrawal of Jesus into the 'not-yet' of what is still to come.

Ascension also implies arrival—the arrival of the Holy Spirit and of Christ's presence and power in him. The ascended Christ has a God-directed ministry as Intercessor (Rom. 8:34; Heb. 7:25), a world-directed ministry as Lord (Eph. 1:21–22), but he has also a Church-directed ministry in the distribution of his power and gifts upon his people. This is clearly seen to be the purpose of the ascension in Ephesians 4:8, "When he ascended on high he led a host of captives and gave gifts to men . . . And his gifts were that some should be apostles, some prophets, some evangelists, some pastors and teachers, for the equipment of the saints, for the work of the ministry, for building up the body of Christ."

This statement is simply a fuller development in the light of the Church's experience, of the initial connection between ascension and Pentecost established in Acts 1:8, before the event, and in Acts 2:33 after it. The ascension as the final stage in Jesus' going away to the Father, constitutes him as the one who has, on the ground of his sacrifice, received from the Father the promised Holy Spirit, and so become the necessary mediator of the Spirit from the Father to the Church. It is in this pouring out of the Spirit that he fulfils his promise to be with the Church to the end of the age (Matt. 28:20). He establishes in the Spirit such fellowship with his people that they have real participation in his ascended life, both in internal reality and in outward manifestation, and yet, because he himself remains transcendent over his fellowship with them, he still confronts them as Lord.

The tension between the here and now of Christ's identification with his people and the eschatological transcendence of the Lord as Judge over his people, has tended to be resolved in different ways by the Catholic and Protestant traditions.

In Catholic tradition the presence of Christ in the Church has been so emphasised as almost to create a merging and identity between them, so that the life of the Church could be thought of as the continuation in earthly history of the life of Christ—the prolongation of the Incarnation. In the same way the teaching of the Church could without qualification be identified with the gospel, and the sense of Christ as transcendent to the Church, as the Judge of her life, of the scriptural gospel as the norm of truth set over and against her own tradition, of the sovereignty of Christ in giving the Spirit, so that the Spirit is by no means the possession of the Church or at the disposal of the Church—all this could be lost sight of in a complacent and unambiguous identification of the Lord with his people.

On the other hand in the more Protestant traditions, the sense of the sovereign majesty of Christ as ascended Saviour and coming

Judge, and the much more sober estimate of the Church as the company of justified sinners, whose sanctification is at best very incomplete—has sometimes led to a feeling of distance and remoteness of Christ from his people, and a failure to realise and act out of the closeness of relationship that being in Christ involves. The objective thoughts of theology have often loomed larger than the life of prayer and fellowship. The ascension of Christ can be seen as his withdrawal into heavenly glory, with all his work ended, so that the burden of his cause and mission falls upon the human shoulders of his people. The way is thus opened for the activist emphasis of so much Protestantism, the pressure of all that we have to do for him, of his dependence upon us, and of our responsibility to bring in his kingdom for him.

If that looks like a parody of any respectable Protestant position, it is an all too accurate description of the practical assumption on which many Protestant congregations—by no means all of them with a liberal label—have been run.

So in terms of II Corinthians 3:18, Protestants have to remember that we do not merely behold the glory of the Lord, but that by the Spirit and through faith we are being changed here and now into a real reflected likeness of that glory. At the same time Catholics have to be reminded that the likeness is not the same as the original and constantly needs to be exposed to it afresh, and that the process of transformation, though real, is partial and incomplete, so that the life of the Church continually needs to be renewed in order to be brought into nearer conformity with the life of the Lord.

In the charismatic renewal, as in other places today, these two traditions are being exposed to each other in a new openness, so that what is of the Spirit in the one can meet what is of the Spirit in the other. One of the things that has greatly impressed me about the Church of the Redeemer in Houston, Texas, is the combination in its life and worship of an intense sense of our corporate identification with Christ as the members of his Body, and an equal sense of his continued sovereign transcendence as divine

Lord. The strong Catholic sense of his immanence was constantly being corrected by the Protestant sense of his Lordship, which in turn was rescued from its remoteness and distance. The Spirit uses us to correct one another and to teach us both to share life with our brother and submit ourselves to the correction of our Judge.

As Karl Barth puts it,

> The Holy Spirit is the power, and his action the work, of the co-ordination of the being of Jesus Christ and that of his community, as distinct from and yet enclosed within it. The Holy Spirit constitutes and guarantees the unity of the *totus Christus* . . . in which he is at one and the same time the Heavenly Head with God and the earthly body with his community. This co-ordination and unity is the work of the active grace of God . . . The freedom of God and his action and operation should not be overlooked or forgotten for a single moment, when we venture, as we must, to see and confess Jesus Christ as the same on both sides, as the Head at the right hand of the Father, and as the Body in the being of the community in its temporal and spatial present and situation, and therefore as the Lord in his totality. (4)

These considerations confront us with a factor in this whole situation which has been implicit throughout, but has not yet come to full expression. The earthly workshop of the Holy Spirit, the place where the glory of Christ is reflected, is the corporate community of Christians. Not the individual 'I' but the corporate 'we' are being changed into Christ's likeness. What the Spirit does personally in each, has its full significance only in relation to what he is doing corporately. The appointed witness to Christ risen and ascended is his Body, the Church, of which individuals are the members, the building into which individuals are to be built together as living stones. The Holy Spirit makes us witnesses by joining and co-ordinating us together in a shared life of strong relationships and ordered ministries of various gifts.

To be called to Christ is by definition to be called to fellowship with those who are called with us. It was so in Galilee, it was so at Pentecost and it is so now. The Holy Spirit, as well as reflecting the character and the power of Christ in Christians, is also concerned with the creation of *koinonia*, the fellowship of a shared life, which will bind them together in one Body, subordinated to the Head and ordered in love with one another.

This is the role specifically assigned to the Spirit in the form of blessing in 2 Corinthians 13:13, where the third in the familiar triad, is the "*Koinonia* of the Holy Spirit". Commentators argue about how the genitive should be taken, whether Paul is praying that the Corinthians should share in the Holy Spirit, or should know that shared life together, which the Holy Spirit creates. The difference between the two is more apparent than real, because in the New Testament any real participation in the Spirit is bound by its very nature to involve commitment to the Christian fellowship which the Spirit creates.

The best illustration of this is the events of the day of Pentecost itself. In Acts 2:3–4 there is recorded an intensely personal *koinonia* —participation in the Holy Spirit, "And there appeared to them tongues as of fire, distributed and resting on each one of them. And they were all filled with the Holy Spirit." But before the chapter has ended that experience has worked itself out in a startlingly corporate way, "And all who believed were together and had all things in common; and they sold their possessions and goods and distributed them to all, as any had need" (Acts 2:44–45).

We may argue about the permanent validity of the particular form which this first venture in Christian community took, but there is no doubt that here we have an authentic work of the Holy Spirit binding people together in a Body as they are bound to Christ, the Head of that Body. Further we can see that as the work of the Spirit is never docetic in its form, so what is created here is not merely some inner and invisible and almost indefinable 'Christian fellowship' or 'spiritual unity', but that the deep internal unity finds practical and indeed financial expression in the sharing of possessions to which it gives rise. Along with the mighty rushing winds at the beginning of the chapter and Peter's sermon and its results in the middle, witness is given to Christ's resurrection by the visible form that the life of his people begins to take—and all these alike are the creations of the Spirit.

It is fascinating to see how the contemporary movement for charismatic renewal has repeated the same process that we have traced in Acts 2. Within eight years my colleague Michael Harper wrote his book, *As at the Beginning*, to commend the experience of Acts 2:4, and his more recent book, *A New Way of Living* to commend a contemporary rediscovery of the *koinonia* described in Acts 2:44. This is symptomatic of the shift from the merely individual to the fully corporate which has taken place within the present movement. If the watchword used to be tongues, now it is community, and many are exploring new ways for Christians to live together and are seeking to share persons, purses and problems, trusting to the Spirit to provide the love that makes it possible.

There can be no doubt at all that such communities are, with all the other works of the Spirit, signs to the Church and to the world of the contemporary activity of the ascended Christ. The world's chief problem is that people do not know how to live together on any level, including the economic; the Church's patchwork efforts at institutional unity have been largely frustrating and disillusioning. Both are bound to take notice when Christians begin to join together in a shared life which proves that in the power of the Spirit incompatible people can be adjusted to one another, so that they can provide a strong corporate base for pastoral care and ministry such as the churches have not often known. For all its possible and actual deviations and exaggerations, the movement to discover new forms of Christian community life is one of the most hopeful on the contemporary scene, and one of the most significant ways in which the likeness of Christ is being expressed among us.

Of course, it is as true of the corporate expression of Christ as it is of the personal, that all must be of the Spirit. The community life of Christians can fall into legality and carnality just as easily as the individual. The experience of religious communities down the ages reminds us that being together is no guarantee of being in the Spirit, and that imitative conformity and unreality can take over here as elsewhere.

It is of vital importance that Christians today should not be imitative of others in the adoption of a communitarian way of life, and there should be no attempt to make what has been a gift of grace and a work of the Spirit in one place a universal law to be imposed from without on every place. The result can only be the loss of the liberty of the Spirit in a new law, and the loss of the creativity of the Spirit in a contradictory charismatic conformity. But where the *koinonia*, whatever its particular form, is given by the Spirit, we have the essential background against which the gifts of the Spirit may operate and the fruits of the Spirit may grow.

In the New Testament both sanctification and charismatic empowering are essentially corporate in character. The fruit of the Spirit is less a catalogue of individual virtues, than the forms of relationship that bind together the Body of Christ; the gifts of the Spirit are less individual endowments, far less spiritual status symbols, than ways in which we work together within the Body of Christ. The "love, joy, peace, patience, kindness, goodness, faithfulness, gentleness, self-control" of Galatians 6:22, 23, are descriptions of the way we relate together in the Church, so that our relationships manifest Christ.

So in Romans 12 and I Corinthians 12, when he is dealing with gifts in the Body, Paul stresses equally the unity of the Body and the variety of the gifts in its various members, "For as in one body we have many members, and all the members do not have the same function, so we, though many are one body in Christ and individually members one of another. Having gifts that differ according to the grace given to us, let us use them" (Rom. 12:4–6). The unity of the Body and the diversity of the gifts are both alike the work of the Spirit, who expresses the love of Christ by drawing the members together, and at the same time expresses the creativity of Christ by realising endlessly new potentialities within them, for the common good and for a witness to Christ. Thus, for example in I Corinthians 14 the gift of prophecy is prized, because, on the one hand, it "edifies the Church" by speaking to men "for their upbuilding encouragement and consolation" (v. 3) and, on the other hand, it reveals God, "But if all prophesy, and an unbeliever or outsider enters, he is called to account by all, the secrets of his heart are disclosed, and so, falling on his face, he will worship God and declare that God is really among you." (vv. 24–25).

If the gifts are employed apart from the unity of the Body, and outside the context of the Church, they become divisive and contentious, as they did at Corinth, and if the Church so defines and institutionalises its unity as to suppress the gifts and quench the Spirit, then the Church goes so far unedified and Christ so far unrevealed. Those whose particular care is for the unity of the Body need to watch that they do not achieve it by suppressing the Spirit, and those whose great desire is for the release of the creative Spirit need to make sure that the end of the upbuilding of the Body is held firmly in view.

All this has implications for both ministry and worship. The nature of the Spirit's operation requires that the wholeness of ministry should belong to the whole Body and not to any one member of it. In the New Testament there is no trace of the omnicompetent ministers our churches are always seeking, but there is a promise of an omnicompetent congregation. To the troublesome Corinthians Paul makes the quite extraordinary statement, "In every way you were enriched in him (Christ) with all speech and knowledge . . . so that you are not lacking in any spiritual gift (*charisma*) as you wait for the appearing of our Lord Jesus Christ" (1 Cor. 1:7)—this was written to a congregation in whom "not many of you were wise according to worldly standards, not many were powerful, not many were of noble birth" (v. 26). But among this bunch of nobodies the Spirit released every gift that they needed to be Christ's people in that place, and this is the norm for the Church. There is certainly a presiding ministry in every congregation, whose calling is to regulate its whole life, but that calling is not to one man to do everything himself, but rather to unlock the potential charisms in all the brethren and recognise and nurture the ministry of the whole Body because "To each is given the manifestation of the Spirit for the common good" (1 Cor. 12:7). The much talked of ministry of the laity has a hope of becoming reality in the freedom of the released Spirit.

The same holds true of the worship; there is an order, a unity, a liturgy in the worship of the Church, which needs to be preserved, and yet can be saved from becoming stereotype and bondage when within the ordered worship, "when you come together, each one has a hymn, a lesson, a revelation, a tongue or an interpretation" (1 Cor. 14:25) and the monotony of the single voice is broken by the ordered spontaneity of corporate Spirit-led worship. Many who have been bored with our services have found in such worship blessing and joy.

Thus, the same Spirit who empowers and sanctifies his people, also draws them together in order that the risen Head may express himself bodily in that corporate new man that is being made in the likeness of the last Adam, the ultimate Man, so that the ascended Lord may be made "head over all things for the Church, which is his body, the fullness of him who fills all in all" (Eph. 1:22–23).

Jesus and Tongues

As AN appendix to this chapter, in which we have been dealing with the relationship of the Spirit to the risen and ascended Jesus, it is as well to draw attention, as we promised, to a minor difficulty in carrying through with complete consistency our general thesis, that what came to the Church at Pentecost was a reflection of what the Spirit had already done in the manhood of Christ.

For among the phenomena of Pentecost was the gift of tongues, "They were filled with the Holy Spirit, and began to speak in other tongues as the Spirit gave them utterance" (Acts 2:4). Now there is no evidence in the Gospels or elsewhere that the gift of tongues had its place, as most of the others did, in the life and ministry of Jesus, and any attempts to locate it there are, in my view, based on evidence so flimsy as to be quite inconclusive.

The personal prayer life of Jesus is covered with a veil of almost unbroken reticence, so that no conclusion about the possible place of tongues in it can, one way or the other, be drawn. In fact the only direct connection between Jesus and the gift of tongues which can be established from the Gospels is the promise in the longer ending of Mark that among the signs which "accompany those who believe" is that "they will speak in tongues" (Mark 16:17–18).

In Acts we are on stronger ground. Jesus is explicitly said to be the source of what the crowds "see and hear" (Acts 2:33), part of

134

which was the tongues of the apostles. Further, those who spoke in tongues are said to be "telling in our own tongues the mighty works of God" (v. 11), which is to be understood as referring to God's mighty works in the resurrection of Jesus. Compare with this Acts 10:46. So also in I Corinthians 12:4–7 tongues are among the variety of gifts that the Spirit imparts, the variety of services the same Lord initiates, the variety of workings the same God inspires.

Thus we can say that, although the gift of tongues is less directly related than some of the other gifts to the human experience of Jesus, yet both in Acts and in Paul it is accepted as functioning within the Christological context of the whole work of the Spirit.

To this can be added the testimony of experience with this gift, that it fits into a Christocentric setting exceedingly well. By it a man edifies himself (1 Cor. 14:4) in the precise sense of being built up as a member of the Body of Christ and brought into a new sense of the Lord's presence. If it did not do that, it would not qualify at all as a gift of the Spirit. The Christological standard applies here as well.

Short of a full treatment of the gift of tongues, which lies outside our present theme, we would simply maintain that, in spite of the gaps in the scriptural evidence, the gift has Christological relevance because in our speaking with tongues Christ is praised and glorified from the bottom of our hearts, so that this gift also has its own place among the ways in which the Spirit mediates Christ to his people.

As John Taylor reports, "Almost all those who have described to me their experience of this gift put their emphasis on the far more vivid awareness it has brought them of God and of Jesus Christ, of the world around, and especially of what other people are feeling, saying and needing." (5) This gift also is a way of being set free by Christ and for Christ in the power of the Spirit.

NOTES
1   F. J. Leenhardt, *The Epistle to the Romans* (Lutterworth), p. 37
2   James D. G. Dunn, "I Corinthians 15:45" in *Christ and Spirit in the New Testament* (Cambridge University Press), pp. 131, 133
3   John V. Taylor, *The Go-Between God* (S.C.M.), p. 213
4   Karl Barth, *Church Dogmatics* (T. & T. Clark), IV, 3, pp. 760, 762

Appendix
5   John V. Taylor, *The Go-Between God* (S.C.M.), p. 218

CHAPTER TEN

By Whatever Name—Receive!

THE TASK which we set ourselves is now nearly complete. We have traced in outline the work that the Spirit of God has done in the ultimate Man, Jesus Christ, in his birth, baptism, temptation, ministry, death and resurrection, until in his ascended glory, he becomes "life-giving Spirit" to his earthly Body. We have seen how by the Holy Spirit, the likeness of his new born, baptised, spirit-filled, crucified, enlivened, and exalted manhood is reflected in those who by faith are turned towards him with unveiled face.

We shall be led to the questions that remain to be asked, if we try to discover where these insights have brought us in terms of the debate about the work of the Holy Spirit that, very creatively, is going on around and within the contemporary charismatic renewal. We might even try to crystallise most of the questions in one question: In the light of the Christological account we have given of the work of the Holy Spirit in Christ and Christians, what precisely do we mean, if we continue to speak of Christians being baptised in the Holy Spirit?

This is of course the controversial phrase round which the argument rages, and that all the books examine almost *ad nauseam*, till one hesitates to join in, and wonders if there is anything fresh or illuminating that can be said on the subject. I do not propose to survey the whole battlefield, but simply to discover what position

on it I should feel happiest about occupying, and how I would
deal with the most immediate attacks that are likely to be made
upon it. It is in some ways a rather exposed position. We have
refused to wear the uniform of a second blessing theology, and the
question is therefore whether we can, without being shot down,
continue to fly a 'baptism in the Spirit' banner!

As I have already indicated at the end of chapter three, I propose to give a positive answer to that question, and will suggest a
definition of baptism in the Spirit which attempts to show that we
can, with a good conscience, go on using the phrase in a way that
incorporates the insights of our study, and that is basically
orientated to what the New Testament says about the Holy Spirit.

But, to set the matter in its right proportion, we should first
make it quite clear that the charismatic renewal does not stand or
fall by the correctness of its exegesis and use of this single New
Testament metaphor. The verbal phrase "to be baptised in the
Spirit" is used six times in the New Testament and is only one
metaphor among many to describe the release of the Spirit among
Christians.

To remain within the first two chapters of Acts, the experience
of Pentecost is variously described as receiving "the promise of
the Father" (Acts 1:4), "being baptised with the Holy Spirit" (v. 5),
"receiving power when the Holy Spirit has come upon you" (v. 8),
"being filled with the Spirit" (Acts 2:4), a "pouring out of the
Spirit" (v. 17), "by the exalted Christ" (v. 33). To assign different
meanings to each of these phrases, as some Pentecostals do,
seems to me impossibly pedantic; they are instructive and mutually
corrective metaphors, all of which Luke uses to describe different
facets of the incomprehensible thing that has happened to the
apostles.

Furthermore, the creative and charismatic activity of the Spirit
is apparent throughout the New Testament, where none of these
formulae is used to describe it. Throughout this book, we have
tried to show that the charismatic dimension of the Spirit's work
does not depend upon a few special phrases or incidents in Acts,

but is integral to the whole New Testament grasp of the work of Christ. When Paul speaks in Ephesians 1:19 of "The immeasurable greatness of Christ, of his power in us who believe" and prays in Ephesians 3:20 to "him who by the power at work within us is able to do far more abundantly than all that we can ask or think," he uses none of the Pentecostal clichés, and does not even speak of the Spirit, but clearly says in principle everything that charismatics want to see recognised in the life of the Church.

There could be nothing more ridiculous than for Pentecostals to insist on a single phrase as the one necessary description of the spiritual experience whose recovery they seek for the whole Church; or for non-Pentecostals to think, that in exposing the theological inadequacies of talk about spiritual baptism, they have somehow disposed of the whole charismatic challenge. It is an old device of the devil to keep Christians out of God's blessing by diverting all their energy (and sometimes venom) into arguing about how they will describe it. Even if the phrase 'baptism in the Spirit' were abolished and banished tomorrow, the invitation to Christians to open themselves up to all that the Spirit wants to do in them would remain as actual and as urgent as ever.

There are in fact influential and sympathetic voices urging us to such an abandonment. Canon Michael Green, writing in *Renewal* magazine, says that to call the new experience of the Spirit, whose validity he accepts, by the name baptism in the Holy Spirit "will not stand up to New Testament teaching and is perhaps the most divisive single factor in the whole (charismatic) movement at present. Could we not bear to call the rose by some other name? It will smell just as sweet." (1) So also the Church of Scotland Panel on Doctrine Report "questions the continuing use of the phrase 'baptism in the Holy Spirit'" (2) as does Archbishop Michael Ramsey, in his foreword to John Gunstone's book *Greater things than these* (3), and it would be unrealistic to pretend that these are not representative of a large body of opinion in the Church.

The objections to the phrase spring of course not from its

biblical use but from its use in Pentecostalism. Its setting seems so irretrievably to be in second blessing theology, that its use almost automatically suggests a two-stage theory of salvation and two accompanying baptisms—a baptism in water into Christ for the remission of sins, and a subsequent baptism in the Holy Spirit imparting power for service.

Now we have ourselves rejected as firmly as we can the two-stage theory of salvation, insisting that the Holy Spirit brings us what is ours in Christ, and not what is beyond Christ. We have presented the outpouring of the Spirit as an integral part of the one baptismal initiation of Christ into his Messiahship and so of Christians into their Christianity. We are therefore in essential theological agreement—at least on the negative side—with Canon Green and the Panel on Doctrine, and the question therefore remains whether we shall accept their recommendation and renounce the baptism in the Spirit language also.

If we are reluctant to do so it is for two significant reasons. First, mainly because we still remain convinced that the New Testament uses the phrase to describe the distinctive experience of the Spirit that came to the Church on the day of Pentecost and, therefore, its use in modern charismatic circles has more basis than many allow, and that many objections to it spring from theological conceptions of water-baptism or conversion which themselves need to be subjected to very careful New Testament scrutiny. Secondly, whatever Canon Green and others may wish, the rose *is* known by this name, and whatever more accurate nomenclature the theological botanists may propose, this is how it is going to continue to be known by thousands of people, and it would seem more pastorally responsible to examine the nature of the flower and of the soil in which it is rooted, than to alter its name. One cannot refrain from adding that the things that the Church has said about water-baptism down the centuries have hardly, to put it mildly, been noted for their puritanical adherence to the New Testament use of *that* phrase. The Pentecostal talk of baptism in the Spirit can claim to be far better related to its New Testament original than much that is said about baptism in water among us.

I would therefore want to maintain that baptism in the Spirit is one legitimate description among others of the Pentecostal experience, and I would like to propose, and then comment upon, the following definition of it. Baptism in the Holy Spirit is that aspect of Christian initiation in which, through expectant and appropriating faith in Christ's promises, the indwelling Holy Spirit manifests himself in our experience, so that he works in and through us with freedom and effecti   ıs he first worked with complete freedom and full effectiveness in the manhood of Christ.

The main comments are as follows:

1   We should note first that the *context* of baptism in the Spirit is Christian initiation. There is no question here of a second initiation, but only of an integral element in the first. Baptism in the Spirit has its place in the complex event of our initiation into Christ, which has as its presupposition the event of new birth and regeneration, which expresses itself in confession of faith and repentance, and receives the justification secured at the Cross, the status of sonship that joins a man to God's family, the Church, and whose sacramental enactment is baptism in water.

In the whole of this complex event, as we have seen, the Holy Spirit is active. It is he who regenerates, who opens to faith and repentance, who witnesses that we are sons, who makes real to us our justification and joins us in the *koinonia*, fellowship of the Church. Thus no man can be initiated into the realm of Christ without at the same time 'having' the Holy Spirit (Rom. 8:9)—i.e. being in the realm where the Spirit is active in him.

It is in this context and this context only that we are to speak of baptism in the Spirit. We are in harmony with the Church of Scotland Report when it says, "Within the context of neo-Pentecostalism, therefore, it is important that if the phrase 'baptism in the Holy Spirit' is to continue in use to describe the essential charismatic experience, it must not be allowed to sever its necessary connection with water-baptism" (4) and with James

Dunn, "The gift of the Spirit may not be separated in any way from conversion . . . The gift of the Spirit, that is, Spirit-baptism, is a distinct element within conversion-initiation." (5) In the New Testament witness, to be baptised in the Spirit is something which normally happens, not in segregation from, or subsequence to our initiation into Christ, upon the fulfilment of special conditions, but as part and parcel of our baptism into the one Lord.

2 But we have to ask not just about the *context*, but about the *content* of baptism in the Spirit. What does it mean? Is it simply another way of describing the activity of the Spirit in regenerating, justifying accepting us into Christ, or does it point to a distinctive aspect of the Spirit's work, closely connected but not identical with these others?

At this point we can make use of the helpful distinction drawn by David C. K. Watson, when he says that in the New Testament the word baptised means both 'initiated into' and 'overwhelmed by'. Thus some hold that to be baptised in the Spirit means simply to be initiated into Christ—into the sphere where the Spirit regenerates, illuminates, sanctifies, so that the phrase describes an initiated status that belongs to every Christian. If this is so, then the argument is over, and all Christians are by definition baptised in the Spirit, because in all of them the Spirit of Christ is working, and Canon Green's rose will have to find a new name.

But others insist that the promised baptism consists of what Watson describes as "an overwhelming of the Spirit, an overwhelming of the love and power of God which so strongly transformed the timid disciples that on and on they went, rejoicing, praising, witnessing. Nothing could stop them, not just because of the theological fact of their Christian initiation, but because of the overwhelming of the Spirit in terms of their personal experience." (6)

If our phrase can have those two distinct meanings, and if some of the confusion is caused because different people are using it in these two different ways, we have to go back to source and ask which it means in the New Testament.

It seems to me that in the New Testament the essential content of the expression, to be 'baptised in the Spirit' is the experience of the released power and energy of the Spirit. Those to whom it happens are regenerated men, who confess Christ as Lord, have their sins forgiven and are accepted as sons, and in all that the Spirit has been at work—but to say that they are baptised in the Spirit refers not specifically to any of that, but rather to the release of the Spirit in power and love and charismatic manifestation within and through them.

This is at least implicit in the saying of John the Baptist, "He will baptise you with the Holy Spirit and with fire" (Luke 3:16) and it becomes explicit in Acts 1:5 where Jesus identifies the fulfilment of John's promise with Pentecost. Pentecost is of course the dispensational sending of the Spirit to do his whole new work in the whole new Church, but it is also the experiential infilling of these apostles by the Holy Spirit, and it is presented, to use David Watson's language again, as an "overwhelming by the Spirit" rather than as a conferring of Christian status upon the apostles.

In spite of the attempt by F. D. Bruner, with what seems to me rather unconvincing help from Acts 11:17, to interpret Acts 2 as the account of the apostles' conversion, the narrative as presented will just not bear that reading. This is not the account of men being regenerated from unbelief into faith, or saved from guilt into forgiveness, or from sin into sanctification. All these are the presuppositions of what happens, but what is actually described is their entering into an overwhelming experience of the manifested presence and power of the Lord through the Holy Spirit, to give them boldness and ability to witness in word and deed in ways that could be seen and heard. This, not regeneration or sanctification, is the focus of their being baptised or filled with the Spirit. It has to do with manifestation rather than relation, witnessing act rather than ethical disposition.

James Dunn tends to play down the experienced empowering of the apostles as being somehow less than central to the event of Pentecost. He argues that in the New Testament the phrase to be baptised in the Holy Spirit is "never directly associated with the promise of power, but is always associated with entry into the Messianic age or the Body of Christ". (7) I suppose that it depends on what you mean by "directly associated", but I would have thought that Acts 1:5, "You shall be baptised with the Holy Spirit" was clearly explicated in Acts 1:8, "You shall receive power", and that the event which fulfilled both was in fact an outpouring of Messianic *power* upon the apostles.

Dunn goes even further, "It is true that when the Spirit thus entered a life in the earliest days of the Church, he regularly manifested his coming by charismata, and his presence by power (to witness), but these were corollaries to his main purpose—the 'Christing' of the one who had taken the step of faith." (8) We may ask in what this 'Christing' essentially consists if witnessing with power is a mere corollary to it. One quite essential element of being 'Christed' is to be brought into an experience of the Spirit's anointing which is analogous to Christ's own, so that as the Father sent him, we in turn may be sent on his service. Witness to Christ, the manifestation of Christ's kingdom and glory is not in the New Testament a corollary to something else more essential. Our being brought into relationship with Christ is in essential connection with our being sent forth by him (Mark 3:14). Our justification and sanctification are for the express purpose that Christ's glory may be manifest among us. Witness is not some corollary to personal salvation, but the end towards which it looks, and therefore our enduement with the power of the Spirit is an essential element in our dynamic relationship with the Lord.

So in Acts 12:16 Cornelius is said to have been baptised in the Spirit, not because he confessed his faith and repented, and so was regenerate (although all that is in the context) but on the ground that "The Holy Spirit fell on them just as on us at the beginning," that they were immersed and overwhelmed by the Spirit's power and he began to manifest his gifts.

Thus all the examples of the use of the phrase seem to me to point to its describing, not simply the activity of the Spirit in relating us to Christ, but to the specific activity of Christ in releasing the Spirit in our conscious experience—and all this as a distinctive part of what it is to be a normal New Testament Christian.

I wonder if it helps us to understand the elusive I Corinthians 12:13, to suggest that in it Paul is holding the two elements we have distinguished in unity, "For by one Spirit we were all baptised into one body"—that is our initiation into Christ in connection with our baptism in water, "and all were made to drink of one Spirit"—that is our experiential participation in the Spirit's presence and power, as a part of what our initiation opens to us.

We should none of us perhaps be too dogmatic at this point. I would myself be content to quote John Taylor's very moderate conclusion, "Students of the New Testament differ in their exegesis; but so far my own reading of it convinces me that the Pentecostalist is right when he calls the bestowal of this gift Baptism in the Holy Spirit. But I think that he is distorting the evidence when he teaches that this is something subsequent to and distinct from becoming a Christian." (9)

In other words, the context is baptismal initiation, but within that context our baptism in the Spirit is that aspect of our life in Christ, in which the Holy Spirit breaks through into our experience, so that we know ourselves to be empowered and gifted to be his witnesses, given a love and a power that do not come from ourselves, but which give us a new appreciation of what it means to belong to Christ and his Body, and new hope and resources to engage in the service to men to which we are called. Those who have known this powerful energising breakthrough of the Spirit into their lives have better backing for their words than is sometimes allowed, when they say that they have been baptised in the Spirit.

We can pinpoint the difference between us and second blessing Pentecostalism by saying that for us the norm of New Testament initiation is Cornelius rather than Samaria. In Cornelius we see the twin promises of Acts 2:38 fulfilled in complete unity with each other. A man is regenerated into such a relationship to Christ that the likeness of Christ in all its evangelical and charismatic aspects begins to appear in him, and the work of the Spirit, from its regenerative mystery to its charismatic expression, is one work of incorporation into Christ. It is a sharing of that Jordan baptism by which the Spirit unites us to Christ in his death, resurrection and anointing. It is such a whole and complete conversion that, as we have already seen, Paul presupposes in the questions he asks at the beginning of Galatians 3, where coming to Christ crucified, receiving the Spirit, and working miracles are not contrasted with one another, or set in some progressive series one after another, but seen in all their togetherness as the one gift and blessing of God in Christ.

In contrast with that, Samaria records a defective situation. A double reception is not the New Testament norm, but merely the New Testament remedy. When the apostles, Peter and John, come to Samaria, they come with an expectation which they find partially unfulfilled. A baptism has taken place which is not a normative baptism, precisely because it has not been a baptism in the Holy Spirit, for the Spirit "had not yet fallen on any of them but they had only been baptised in the name of the Lord Jesus" (Acts 8:16).

James Dunn is, to my mind, at his least convincing in his treatment of this incident (10) when he argues, on rather meagre grammatical evidence, that the Samaritans, in spite of having believed and been baptised under the ministry of Philip, were not Christians before Peter and John arrived. He is forced into this position by his insistence that the bestowal of the Spirit by the laying on of the apostles' hands must mean that bestowal which regenerates us and constitutes our relationship to Christ, so that, until the Spirit fell, there was only intellectual assent to Philip's teaching and no real commitment to Christ.

It is hard to make the story read this way. We need only point to the different treatment accorded by Peter to the mass of the Samaritan believers and to Simon Magus. With the former, he accepted their faith and baptism as valid, though incomplete.

There is no suggestion that he identified in them, anything analogous to Simon's bitter heart of unbelief, that would have rendered their response to Philip's ministry null and void. On the contrary, the bestowal of the Spirit did not constitute their initiation into Christ, but rather fulfilled it.

I much prefer Beasley-Murray's suggestion that in Acts 8, Luke is "describing a Church in which the Spirit was not unknown, but in which the Spirit's gifts were not yet manifest . . . It is clear that the laying on of hands by Peter and John, accompanied by their prayer for their lack to be made good, was at once followed by the impartation of the charismata." (11) In other words, the Spirit was already active in the baptism and the believing, the validity of which the apostles tacitly accept, but there was a receiving of the Spirit which was not regenerative, but which showed itself in a new release of the Spirit in freedom, power and gifts. This release of the Spirit was so integral to the 'Christing' of the Samaritans that their baptism, though effective and real, was incomplete without it, and remedial measures for its completion had to be adopted. This laying on of hands is not to bring them into some second spiritual baptism, distinct from their baptism in water, it is to release the Spirit to act in them in a way consistent with their position in Christ as baptised believers. What happened in Samaria was not standard, but rather the story of how the Christian subnormal was brought up to standard.

3   We consider now the *conditions* for being baptised in the Spirit. In the account of the defective Christians at Samaria, we are offered no explanation why they were unable to enter into a complete possession of their baptismal blessings, and all the elaborate explanations that have been suggested at this point belong very much to the realm of not always disinterested speculation.

When, however, we come to the current situation in the contemporary Church, we are not left to speculate about why the baptised believers in our day have in very many cases not entered into the experience of the power of Christ released among them, and why therefore they stand in need, not of a second initiation, but of a fresh experience of the extent and magnitude of the operations of the Holy Spirit who is already at work within them.

The answer is that in the teaching and expectation of the churches in most of our denominations and doctrinal traditions, this whole aspect of the Spirit's work in equipping the Church for internal fellowship and external mission, has been much muted. The promise of John 14:12 was decidedly *not* something that as a Christian I was told to expect to see fulfilled in the life of the Church, when I committed myself to Christ.

So like ancient Israel, we who by faith in Christ had come out of the house of bondage were nevertheless unable to enter into all of God's promises—because of our unbelief. "So we see that they were unable to enter because of unbelief" (Heb. 3:19). It is this situation of believers who will not believe that we find so often in our churches today. The very people who by faith in Christ have received reconciliation and forgiveness by grace, are closed to the fact that by the same faith in the same gospel and by the same grace, the power of the Spirit of Christ can be released within them and come out from them. By faith they enter into one whole area of scriptural promise, but by unbelief they exclude themselves from another. Thus we have defined the means by which the full freedom of the Spirit becomes possible to us as "expectant and appropriating faith in Christ's promises".

It may seem to some that this sort of approach to the functioning of faith gives it a whole range of objects to which it has to relate itself in an atomistic way, and a whole series of promises which it has to claim one by one, whereas in the New Testament the object of faith seems to be single and simple, and, as F. D. Bruner keeps insisting, all we need is simple faith in Christ in order to inherit all his promises.

This is of course valid in so far as it emphasises that "all the promises of God find their Yes in him" (2 Cor. 1:20), that Christ is the ultimate object of every scriptural promise and that we find every spiritual blessing in him. It is true that if we believe in Christ we do not have to believe in anything else.

But we also need to be clear that the Christ in whom we believe is not a Christ restricted to that area of operation which our own particular brand of Christian tradition allots to him, but rather the whole Christ in the whole range and extent of his Person and Work and of his gospel's offer to us. We have in fact to relate ourselves in faith to the one who is everything indicated by his name, Jesus, Lord, and Christ, who operates on the comprehensive scale indicated in the New Testament, who is therefore not only the lamb of God who takes away the sin of the world but also he who will baptise us with the Holy Spirit and with fire. To adapt J. B. Phillips's famous title, Our Christ has been too small. Or, as Father Simon Tugwell says, "While we may agree with Bruner that Christianity plus is no longer Christianity, Pentecostalism has come in protest against Christianity minus." (12) We are to be open to all of Christ and not dispensationalise away whole vital aspects of the Gospel. Faith is that openness and it has to grow so as to become more and more adequate to its object.

It is still true, of course, that from the very first moment of our believing we are joined in one life with the whole Christ, and charismatic experiences have come to many who have never been exposed to the message of the released fullness of the Spirit. I would have to testify that one of the most outstanding works of healing in my own ministry happened when I had never considered these things in any serious way. But I was a Christian man and joined to Christ, in principle therefore open to charismatic gifts, so that in the occasional and untypical moments of openness to his power, he was able to work through me. But, most of the time I did not then believe in these particular possibilities of his released power in any expectant way, so that the Spirit was so far quenched and Christ so far limited in what he did through me. When I became open in principle to his promises of power, the Spirit was then able to enter through a more widely open door and to manifest his presence and power in ways that unbelief had up till that point greatly impeded.

In our definition we used the term 'appropriating faith'. This is language to which F. D. Bruner takes the strongest exception, "It is our impression that 'appropriation' has been the mother of more conditions, if not more misery than any other word we have encountered in Pentecostalism ... The notion of appropriation tends to make the believer's faith even more central than God's gift, or, to put it another way, to make faith a work." (13)

Bruner is here indicating real dangers, and some Pentecostal treatments of faith may merit his strictures. But I do not accept that the whole notion of appropriation is as man-centred and Arminian as he makes out, and would claim that on the contrary it does represent a real element in the New Testament teaching about faith.

Bruner's chief fear is that faith should become a 'human work'. Now a work, in this theological sense, may be defined as that which (a) has its source in man and (b) in virtue of its own intrinsic quality is the ground on which God bestows his blessing as its reward. The appropriating faith of which we are speaking is not a human work in either of these senses.

(a) It docs not have its source in man. People fail to believe in the whole range of the Spirit's work, not mainly because they are personally defective in faith, but because the gospel that has been declared to them has been defective, and it is the word that creates faith. Faith is the human response which is totally dependent upon and created by the word delivered, "So faith comes from what is heard, and what is heard comes by the preaching of Christ" (Rom. 9:17). Because Christ has not been adequately preached as the bestower of the Spirit, the faith by which he could manifest himself has not been created. The way to create that faith is not to exhort people to it, as though it was within their own power, but to declare the full Christ, which will create faith. Such faith is not a work that stands in opposition to God's free gift, so as to condition its freedom; it is a human response created by the message and so itself part of the gift.

(b) Faith is not the ground on which, but rather the means by which we receive God's blessing. We are not blessed because of the depth or quality of our faith, by the correctness of its theological affirmations or the profundity of its religious feeling. Faith is great, not when it is great in quality or quantity, but when it is great in extent. It may be as small as a grain of mustard seed, but if it is prepared to act on Christ's promise, it may give orders to mountains.

In other words, faith takes its value solely from the object on which it is set; it is because it is openness to Christ in all his reality, that it is the appointed means of his action by the Spirit in our experience.

Faith therefore is not an activity which has its source in man and which, by its own quality, earns God's blessing. It is the human response to the gospel which God creates and uses as the means for bestowing his blessing, so that in its absence that blessing is blocked and cannot freely be bestowed.

But faith is not sheer passivity—this is the positive justification for the word appropriation. Faith is a trusting which has become a taking, it is a believing which does not inertly wait for the blessing to be delivered, but so trusts the reality of the promise made by God, that it stretches out its hand to accept what it sees him offering. Faith is that active obedience by which Peter so trusts Christ's word to him that he lets down his nets on the other side of the boat, and later leaves the boat and puts his weight on the water, by which the heroes of Hebrews 11 proceed to the act that expresses their faith, and so obtain the promises that attach to it.

Jesus expresses this in John 7:37, "If any one is thirsty, let him come to me and *drink*." 'Drinking' is that obedience of faith which says the human 'yes' to God's promise and proceeds to act upon its truth. It does not have its source in itself or its value in itself, but only in the word and presence of Christ. But faced with that word and in that presence, it does not relapse into inactivity, but reaches out and takes what is offered to it. So, in relation to the blessings of the Spirit, we do not simply wait for Christ to bestow them as he will, we earnestly seek them (cf. 1 Cor. 14:1, "Earnestly desire (*zeloute*) the spiritual gifts"), and when we are convinced that he means us to have them we appropriate them, we reckon that they are ours, proceed to act on that assumption, and find that it is so.

Appropriating faith is no human work, but that active human obedience, elicited by God's word, by which his promises are trusted and tested, and by which they pass into experienced fulfilment.

4   We should consider, finally, the particular *nature* of the experi-ence. We have tried to define baptism in the Spirit theologically, that is, in relation to the promise of Christ and in connection with other aspects of the gospel. Mindful of our own earlier warning not to set up a law of spiritual experience, we have kept our own definition at this point quite deliberately unspecific and have been content to say that the Spirit manifests himself in our experience and works in and through us with freedom and effectiveness.

When we compare the experiences of the Spirit described in Acts, we can say that in all of them the Spirit does the same thing differently. The position is exactly parallel to conversion, in which the *how* of its happening is infinitely varied, and yet has as the essential *what* of its happening the trusting and confessing of Christ as Saviour and Lord.

So with our initiation into the liberty of the Spirit, the im-portant question is not the *when*—to which altogether too much attention has been given—or even the *how*, but rather the *what*. And the essential content of the experience is that we should begin to be conscious of the ability and the power of Christ to do in and through us all that he did in and through his own human nature. The particular way in which that happens, and the place it occupies in the timescale of our spiritual progress, will be infinitely varied. Pentecost, Samaria, the experience of Saul, Cornelius and the disciples at Ephesus, were different and yet they all came into a decisively new consciousness of the power of the Spirit of Jesus. So within modern testimony literature, its variety rather than its clichéd uniformity, will persuade us that the Creator Spirit has indeed been at work.

The most prominent feature of the experience for some will be a new sense of closeness to Christ; for others it will be the discovery of a new very specific relevance in the word of Scripture; for others a new urge to pray and reality in prayer; for others a new sense of openness to people and of effective relationship with them; for others an entering into victory at a salient point of moral defeat; and for yet others a new boldness to be Christ's witness, and a new charismatic manifestation. Whatever elements predominate in particular cases, the common factor is that God the Holy Spirit is working in people with a love and power and freedom they have not previously known. The particular experience is significant because it marks a breakthrough into a fresh dimension of their experiential relationship with Christ.

It may be sudden, critical and sensationally transforming; it may be slow and quiet and spread over a period; the Spirit is symbolised by dew as well as by wind, but even when the dew falls silently, it will make the leaves wet and fresh and sweet. Even when the Spirit comes quietly, we shall be aware that he has come, and his manifestation will be known also in the Body of Christ around us.

And, to repeat it again, so that there may be no mistake—as there is no law of experience, so there is no law of tongues. Again and again the gift of tongues is the means by which the Spirit opens the deep places of our personality to a new praise of God and a new availability to people. But that happens, not according to some supposed law of initial evidence, but only according to the royal law of love, by which the Spirit matches this particular provision to our particular need, as he seeks to free our manhood in all its parts to reflect more and more of the manhood of Jesus, and as he works on all the levels of our nature from the most outward and physical to the most inward and spiritual.

And, however and whenever, it happens, not as some advanced degree in an esoteric Christian freemasonry, but as part of what belongs to everyone who belongs to Christ, into which he bids us enter from the very first moment of our coming to him, and from which we are excluded by nothing but our own quenching of the Spirit and our unbelief in the Lord's promises. It took some of us a long time to realise that Christ had all this waiting for us, but as soon as we are ready to believe, we shall discover that from the very first of his dealings with us, the charismatic freedom of the Spirit has been implicit in his offer to us, and to become explicit waits for nothing but our willingness to open ourselves to it.

As the experience itself is not to be legalised or stereotyped in any way, so the language in which we describe it must not be stereotyped either. We have argued that the term 'baptism in the Spirit' when set in its right context is one way in which, in responsibility to Scripture, it can be legitimately described. But there are many others, and the Holy Spirit, amidst all the other realms of his creativity, can be expected to be creative in our theology as well, and as we discuss these things together within the Body of Christ, give us more adequate language with which to depict and praise himself and his work—adequate both to the richness of Scripture and the need and understanding of modern men.

We may share Professor Walter Hollenweger's fear of what will happen to the Pentecostal emphasis if it is to be straightjacketed into an accommodation with classical theology (14), if that means the activity of the Spirit is to be categorised and docketed and robbed of its freedom.

We have tried to avoid that kind of theologising in this book. For we have argued that the outpouring of the Spirit has its meaning, not in terms of any closed system of ideas, or any fixed pattern of experience, but in terms of the Person and work and mission of Christ. The significance of the work of the one divine Person is communication of the other divine Person. The Spirit blows where he wills, the experience and the events that he brings about in the Church and in individuals are infinite in their variety and creativity, but all the work of the Spirit is disciplined and ordered by the magnetic pole to which it is for ever drawn, which is the new manhood of the Lord.

The completion of that work is for the day of Christ's appearing, but its beginning is now, as in his own way the Spirit travails over us that Christ may be formed within us in all the newness of his humanity. He again and again unveils our faces so that we may behold his glory, and reflect it in the corporate re-created humanity of Christ's Body. The great concern of the Spirit is Christ—and Christ in us, which is the hope of glory. (Col. 1:17)

The Greek of 2 Corinthians 9:15, "Thanks be to God for his *dwrea anekdiegeto*", is usually, and quite correctly, rendered 'unspeakable gift' but means literally, 'not fully drawn out gift'. The one complete gift is Christ, the Son of God made man in our flesh by the Holy Spirit, and the work of the Spirit is to draw out of Christ all that is in him for us, so that we may be the preliminary expression of his glory. And all this he does by grace through faith, not so that books may be written about it, but so that it may be received, and that the thanks of the Church may be its faithful reflection of the glory of the Lord. "Thanks be to God for his not-yet-fully-drawn-out gift."

Notes to Chapter Ten

NOTES
1   Michael Green, "Renewal" Fountain Trust No. 53 (October 1974), p. 14.*
2   Report of the Panel on Doctrine, "The Charismatic Movement within the Church of Scotland", (1974), p. 17
3   Michael Ramsey, Foreword to John Gunstone, *Greater Things than These* (Faith Press), p. 7

*Since this chapter was written Michael Green's book *I Believe in the Holy Spirit* (Hodder and Stoughton) has been published. I greatly appreciate his wise and generous assessment of the charismatic renewal, but he has not convinced me that I need to change the interpretation offered in this chapter of what the New Testament means when it speaks of being baptized in the Spirit.

4   Panel on Doctrine, ibid. p. 12
5   James D. G. Dunn, *Baptism in the Holy Spirit* (S.C.M.), p. 226
6   David C. K. Watson, *One in the Spirit* (Hodder & Stoughton), p. 68
7   James D. G. Dunn, ibid. p. 228
8   Ibid. p. 226
9   John V. Taylor, *The Go-Between God* (S.C.M.), p. 199
10 James D. G. Dunn, ibid. pp. 55–68
11 G. R. Beasley-Murray, *Baptism in the New Testament* (Macmillan), p. 119
12 Simon Tugwell, *Did you Receive the Spirit* (Darton, Longman & Todd), p. 83
13 F. D. Bruner, *A Theology of the Holy Spirit* (Hodder & Stoughton), p. 251
14 Walter J. Hollenweger, *The Pentecostals* p. 106

Select Bibliography

A. Theological and Christological Background

Barth, Karl *Church Dogmatics* (T. & T. Clark) Especially I, 2 and IV

Berkouwer, G. C, *The Person of Christ* (Eerdmans)

Bonhoeffer, Dietrich, *Christology* (Collins)

Brunner, Emil, *The Christian Doctrine of the Church, Faith and the Consummation* (Lutterworth)

Irving, Edward *Christ's Holiness in Flesh*
The Sealing Virtue of Baptism
The Opinions Circulating Concerning Our Lord's Human Nature
Facts Connected with Recent Manifestations of Spiritual Gifts

Johnson, Harry *The Humanity of the Saviour* (Epworth)

Kelsey, Morton *Encounter with God* (Hodder and Stoughton)
Healing and Christianity (S.C.M.)

Pannenberg, Wolfhart *Jesus God and Man* (S.C.M.)

Strachan, C. Gordon *The Pentecostal Theology of Edward Irving* (Darton, Longman & Todd)

Torrance, Thomas F. *Theology in Reconstruction* (S.C.M.)

B. The Doctrine of the Spirit and His Gifts

Berkhof, Hendrikus *The Doctrine of the Holy Spirit* (Epworth)

Bittlinger, Arnold *Gifts and Graces* (Hodder and Stoughton)
Gifts and Ministries (Hodder and Stoughton)

Bruner, Frederick Dale *A Theology of the Holy Spirit* (Hodder and Stoughton)

Buchanan, George *The Office and Work of the Holy Spirit* (Banner of Truth)

Dunn, James D. G. *Baptism in the Holy Spirit* (S.C.M.) *Jesus and the Spirit** (S.C.M.)

Green, Michael *I Believe in the Holy Spirit** (Hodder and Stoughton)

Murray, G. R. Beasley *Baptism in the New Testament* (Macmillan)

Schweizer, Eduard *Spirit of God* (translated from Kittel's *Theologisches Worterbuch zum Neuen Teastament*) (Adam & Charles Black)

Smeaton, George *The Doctrine of the Holy Spirit* (Banner of Truth)

Taylor, John V. *The Go-Between God* (S.C.M.)

Torrey, R. A. *The Person and Work of the Holy Spirit* (Zondervan)

Tugwell, Simon *Did You Receive the Spirit*? (Darton, Longman & Todd)

C. The Holy Spirit in the Church Today

Gunstone, John *Greater Things than These* (Faith Press)

Harper, Michael C. *As at the Beginning* (Hodder and Stoughton) *A New Way of Living* (Hodder and Stoughton)

Hollenweger, Walter J. *The Pentecostals* (S.C.M.)

O'Connor, Edward D. *The Pentecostal Movement in the Catholic Church* (Ave Maria Press, Notre Dame, Indiana)

Suenens, Cardinal Leon Joseph *A New Pentecost*?* (Darton, Longman and Todd)

Watson, David C. K. *One in the Spirit* (Hodder and Stoughton)

*These works have been published since the manuscript of this book was completed.